My Big Idea Book

Inspired by Global
Best-Selling Authors

Compiled by Viki Winterton

My Big Idea Book
Inspired by Global Best-Selling Authors

©2016 by Viki Winterton

Expert Insights Publishing
1001 East WT Harris Blvd #247
Charlotte, NC 28213

ISBN-13: 978-1537354422
ISBN-10: 1537354426

Compiled by: Viki Winterton

Cover Design: Terry Z

Edited by: Pam Murphy

15 14 13 12 11 1 2 3 4 5

A portion of the profits from this book will be donated to
Supporting Our Servicemen, an Organization dedicated to
helping and thanking our past and present Veterans.

"How wonderful it is that nobody need wait a single moment before starting to improve the world."
~ Anne Frank

Foreword
By Dr. Klara Gubacs-Collins

There were three factors that brought me to my big idea. Three significant life events really that represented an enormous shift in how I observe and live in the world. One was that as a life-long athlete, I kept failing in trying to complete in, what I named, our country club's "grand slam." Not being able to win the "last leg" was an unknown territory simply because I was used to winning in sports. Not that I won everything in my life but I always performed well in big events that mattered. I had won at tennis, platform tennis as well as the one out of two golf championships, but I just could not complete the last leg, which was the Ladies' Golf Championship.

The main issue was that I "choked" every time when it was tournament time. While I used to always bring my best to the big tests, something kept breaking down in this event. What kept me going was that I do believe when people have a desire to accomplish something then the universe has already provided them with the means to achieve that goal. Therefore, it is up to each individual to find the way to overcome those obstacles and realize their dreams.

Everybody was telling me the last six years, "Oh come on. Why don't you just give up?" I said, "No, because there is something inside me; I know that I was meant to do this." If you wake up every morning dreaming of having a particular goal or achievement, you must not stop in its pursuit, no matter how many people tell you that maybe it's not for you. It may not be worth it for them, but it's worth it to you.

The second life event was about three years ago when I started to get sick. I started to gain weight, became extremely moody, and experienced memory issues and brain fog. Literally "out of the blue." As the weeks progressed, things were getting worse. As my usually very understanding husband put it, I was experiencing PMS 24/7. I have always been a loving and calm person, and I really hated myself for behaving this way. It was just a really awful feeling not having the power to control my emotions.

I was diagnosed with hypothyroidism. My amazing family doctor, who I trust completely, said: "Okay, for the next two months, I can give you medication, and if it doesn't work, then you may have to have surgery." In about one week, I said to the doctor, "Listen, give me a couple of months. Let me see what I can do with myself and how I can solve this issue without medication." Being the forward thinking doctor he was, he agreed and allowed me to change my life without medication. I changed my diet and outlook on life completely and have never turned back.

The third life event was that while I truly, truly love my job as a university professor, because of all that was going wrong in my life, I just could not find pleasure in my profession. Something was affecting that as well. So, at this point in my life, I was blaming the university for changing on me. I was blaming my coaches in the sports for my failing. I couldn't really find anyone to blame for my health issues. It was what I call a perfect storm coming together in my life.

In the midst of this perfect storm, I found energy psychology and inner reconciliation with all its tools, and I never looked back. I started to study and completely dedicate my life to understanding the difference between traditional psychology and energy psychology, and how it affects our lives. I also developed the Winning Mind Blueprint especially for athletes, but really for all who fail when it counts the most. The times when you're trying to break through your limits and become the champion that you truly are while you feel that you're going to choke. You just can't deliver your best. I realized through my years of studies that it is for a completely different reason than what we see on the outside and the majority of mental coaches have approached it from the wrong direction.

I use this blueprint in all aspects of my life, and it has delivered in immense proportions. Last year, I finally won my trophy by overcoming the mental challenges of losing for years, and knowing that while my skills may never measure up to my opponent, my mind has to, and it did. So many of us know we have more inside of us. We can be better, but there's something in our subconscious stopping us. We may be even good now, but we can be great. This is how we go from Contender to Champion!

Then I completely healed myself of every single symptom that I had. Even now, I am amazed by this. Every single symptom I had was gone within a week, just by changing my diet, by changing my routines and habits. In order to change my diet, I had to use energy psychology to help me eliminate the cravings, understanding why I craved certain things and why they had to be eliminated. It was an incredible process. I went back to the doctor about a month later and he was stunned, "Oh my, all your numbers are normal. What happened?" I explained it to him. For me, energy psychology was a tremendous breakthrough even in regaining my health.

Even though my job still gives me some hard times and as the happier and more content I get in my life, the more some people can't stand my happiness. Through my studies, I understood that people who are not fulfilled might still be coming from their "pain body," which stems from the original pain that was instilled in them throughout generations. They also have difficulty accepting that so much of this pain is in the mind as a result of all the stories we develop around life events that happened to us. I know it's hard to believe but a mere human can actually go within and change herself. For example, my relationship with my students has changed immensely. You cannot be an educator and come from pain. You have to come from love, because you have to have this unconditional love for the class that you are teaching, no matter how your students might be "pushing your buttons." You need to know that if a child pushes your button, it's your problem, not theirs. They're not bad children. You have a button to eliminate. As a result, most of my students told me, "You've got to go out into the bigger world and inspire more than just the university crowd," because as they said, I have "it."

My message is about the power of the internal and external healing and completion of recovery to those who are truly ready to get **committed** to change. This is the hardest part for us to do. Why? Because when we decide to change, there are certain aspects in us that we just cannot live with anymore. That is a scary, scary experience. How is it going to affect everything from family relationships to your job to your calling in life?

My biggest idea so far is to bring people to the understanding of two points. One is that the answer to their questions, whatever the question may be, is not outside of them. The answer to their questions, to their problems, to their issues is inside of them. If I could spend the rest of my life with the tools I have pointing people into the direction where I could catalyze their 'ah-ha' moment, *my calling in life would be fulfilled*.

They will have that 'ah-ha' moment of clarity: "Oh, wait. If I get triggered by such-and-such comments, it has nothing to do with the person that made the comment to me. It has to do with an event way back when something, somewhere happened to me. I just built up a defense in regards to that issue or tone of voice, and the outside world hits that button from time to time.

The second point is that my job as a human being is to get to those trigger points, understand them, accept them, and if need be clear them, so I gain the control back in my life instead of giving it to others. Then I am free to choose. If I choose to give some control, as when I got married, I may choose to give some control to someone, but it's my choice. It's not my need. It is so empowering for people to understand the difference between being **vulnerable by need and being vulnerable by choice**. These are basically the points in my big idea and helping people reach this control is my biggest work.

My hope for you is that this journal, *My Big Idea Book* will inspire you to look at possibilities through your desire for what you want to do. Not the how, but what you want to do. Then let your inspiration guide you, because if your inspiration guides you, there are no obstacles or impossible tasks to make your big idea your reality.

To All of Your Big Ideas,

Dr. Klara Gubacs-Collins

Dr. Klara Gubacs-Collins has been teaching at MSU (Montclair State University) in the Department of Exercise Science and Physical Education for over 15 years. She's also a researcher, a "grand slam" winning athlete and a best-selling author.
Connect with her on her website:
https://www.winningmindinstitute.com ,
by email: dr.gubacs@winningmindtherapy.com
or on Facebook:
"The Art of Winning" Group
(www.facebook.com/groups/1583533815280664/)

"With advertising, you pay for it. With publicity, you pray for it. You need all four legs of the publicity chair — print, radio, television and internet.

When you do something just to make money, it is almost always the wrong decision. There's got to be something else driving you. It's got to be fun. You've got to be giving back. You've got to be helping people. If you do that, then the money will follow."

Rick Frishman, Best-Selling Author, Publisher and Speaker, Founder of Author 101 University, the Premier event for marketing and publishing success.   Author101University.com

My Big Idea

My Big Idea

—DAY 2 —

"Speaking is about five major things: The right message, the right market, the right brand, the right marketing materials and the right avenues of promotion. Make sure these five elements are in place to start getting highly paid to speak. Those who win in business and life are the people who offer the most value to others. Want your life to be richer? Ask yourself, "What could I do today to add value to someone's life?"

Mike Fritz, Best-Selling Author, Speaker, Coach and Founder of The Magnetic Speaker Event and Founder of Algorithms for Success. AlgorithmsforSuccess.com

My Big Idea

— _DAY 2_ —

My Big Idea

— DAY 3 —

"Make money fall in love with you.

When you imagine your money as a real, flesh and blood person, worthy of your deepest admiration, you embark on an amazing, love-at-first-sight affair of the heart.

Pennies on the ground are like chocolates on your pillow."

Morgana Rae is a sought after teacher, speaker and pioneer in personal development and is widely regarded to be the world's leading Relationship with Money coach. MorganaRae.com

My Big Idea

— _DAY 3_ —

My Big Idea

— DAY 4 —

"I was warned, 'You're not going to make money selling books. You're going to make money by having a book and using it to close more deals.' That has been my experience—an experience far exceeding my goals and my vision!

When you do what you love, and you do it in the company of visionaries and household names, you become an instant expert in your field. You owe it to the world to get your story out in a book."

Viki Winterton, Publisher, #1 International Best-Selling Author, and Founder of Expert Insights Publishing. ExpertInsightsPublishing.com

My Big Idea

_____

_____

_____

_____

_____

_____

_____

_____

_____

_____

_____

_____

_____

_____

_____

_____

_____

_____

_____

_____

— *DAY 4* —

My Big Idea

"After decades of research, the entire human genome was finally cracked, and genetic science took a giant leap forward.

Epigenetics is the study of biological mechanisms that switch genes on and off without altering our actual DNA.

In other words, through our gene expressions - our diet, fitness, attitude, and outlook - we affect how our cells read our genes to consequently impact our health and wellness. This scientific study has become my life's work."

Dr. Aimon Kopera, MD is a leading global authority on Epigenetics and a constant advocate for easily applying this emerging science to significantly improve our health. KoperaMD.com, DrKopera@iriwp.com

My Big Idea

— _DAY 5_ —

My Big Idea

— DAY 6 —

"Hearing God's voice during the darkest hours of my life, I became accustomed to His outrageous requests. 'Write a book, become a best-selling author, speak in local churches and then the world. Build a home and school for widows and children in India.' Watching my visions and conversations with God manifest daily into reality, I smile. Nothing is impossible for those who walk according to His divine purpose. Thank you God for choosing me."

Karen Bode is a mother, grandmother, international best-selling author, teacher and mentor to women seeking freedom and healing through God using her life's testimony and book, *Clean Heart*.   thePowerfulWomenofGod.org

My Big Idea

— _DAY 6_ —

My Big Idea

— DAY 7 —

"Some people spend their whole life chasing what they already have. They are looking for approval and encouragement. They look everywhere except inside themselves. We use our own words to program our subconscious minds which drives our actions and, eventually, our results. Only we put limits on ourselves. To realize your true potential seek from within. Look no further than yourself. For the sky is the limit. Let your inner drive be the guide."

Rev. Dr. Tracy Elman, D.D., D.M., is a narrator, multi-award winning, best-selling author, and founder of <u>LeapToNewHeights.com</u> Empowerment, Education and Coaching.

My Big Idea

_____
_____
_____
_____
_____
_____
_____
_____
_____
_____
_____
_____
_____
_____
_____
_____
_____

— *DAY 7* —

My Big Idea

— *DAY 8* —

"When one puts forth effort into living an inspired and enlightened life, it can be disconcerting when negative emotion rears up. I believe these times of negativity are an effective gauge to realize how far you have come. When negative emotions appear, you have the opportunity to view them from your new, enlightened perspective. From this place, you can employ new approaches and benchmark the progress you've made."

After failing a high school Creative Writing course, **Kitty A. Smith** never expected to become a writer. The Universe seems to be conspiring against those teachers because she's been drawn to writing despite their disapproval. KittyASmith.com

My Big Idea

— _DAY 8_ —

My Big Idea

— *DAY 9* —

"You cannot truly love another unless you love yourself first. It's just not possible and if you say you do, it's a lie. Everything starts with you. If you attempt to love others when you aren't loving yourself, it's not genuine. Love yourself first because when you do, it's like throwing a pebble in a pond. There's a ripple effect and everyone feels the love and benefits from it. Love yourself first, then it's contagious!!"

Susan D. Wedgewood-Goudy, MSW, and author of
*The Journey From Fear To Love Is Shorter Than **YOU** Think*
teaches people to consciously create a life they'll love.
SusanGoudy.com

My Big Idea

— _DAY 9_ —

My Big Idea

— _DAY 10_ —

"We are coming up to another New Year! Now is the time to plan for what you want. I suggest you select a charity to which you wish to contribute, actually ask them what is the best way you can help make a difference and give back with your time, not just the usual donations. We all need to support each other to experience the bliss of contribution and connection, understand life, heritage and legacy."

Susie Briscoe is the Founding Chair of Acer Coaching Associates, co-author of two #1 Int'l Best-Selling books, Int'l Business Executive Coach/Mentor and Master Leadership with Legacy Mentor. AcerCoachingAssociates.com

My Big Idea

— *DAY 10* —

My Big Idea

"Perseverance is the secret sauce of success. Without it, no great achievement is possible. Even if a person is not very talented or highly knowledgeable but of an average merit, he still can succeed in life simply by his perseverance. Every action has its reaction. So hard labor has no alternative, it must yield results."

Andreas A. Jones is a #1 Int'l Best-Selling Author, Coach, Speaker, Trainer and Army Veteran.   <u>AndreasAJones.com</u>

My Big Idea

— *DAY 11* —

My Big Idea

— DAY 12 —

"It took over half a century for me to learn that self-care is not selfish. Take time for yourself. You cannot be as effective in life when you are feeling depleted. What are some things you can do for yourself physically, emotionally, and spiritually to better support your needs? Reflect upon how you will work those things into your life. Be authentic, do what you love, and be sure to nurture yourself along the journey."

Susan Jeffrey Busen is an Award-Winning Int'l Best-Selling Author, Int'l Speaker, Practitioner, and Founder of the GetSet™ Approach, Tap into Balance, and My Pet Healer. TapintoBalance.com

My Big Idea

— _DAY 12_ —

My Big Idea

"Routine — to some it's comforting and to others it's terrifying — but to everyone it's something that can potentially stand in the way of allowing change to improve your life. So many people in this world are immobilized because they've narrowed their perception and closed so many doors that poised positive change in life. Choose to reopen those doors and welcome all of the spontaneity and infinite experiences that change will bring you."

William Busen studied finance at DePaul University and is an author, world traveler, fitness guru, aspiring entrepreneur, and life enthusiast.   outsideinjournal.com

My Big Idea

— *DAY 13* —

My Big Idea

— _DAY 14_ —

"What makes parting with the loss of any achievement easier is realizing that it might have been your last. Every fortune and misfortune brings forth tremendous growth, which is the very essence of all life! Never allow yourself to feel like a victim of your circumstances. The reality of who we are lies so far beyond our perceptions and boundaries. As you seek to find yourself on this journey, invest in love and forgiveness."

Tom Busen is a writer and LoA Practitioner. After a near fatal motorcycle accident in 2011, his efforts have focused on healing and inspiring others. outsideinjournal.com

My Big Idea

— _DAY 14_ —

My Big Idea

— DAY 15 —

"Our decisions are either dictated by fear or courage. Fear holds us back more than anything. Fear only exists if we allow it. It's our biggest barrier to achieving success. Fear is the reason we resist challenging ourselves and why we quit before we get what we want. Fear causes us to settle while falling short of our true potential. Ask for what you want and don't be afraid to hear the word 'no.'"

Dan Busen is pursuing a Marketing degree at DePaul University. He is a best-selling author, devoted body builder, and motivational thought leader. BusenBros.com

My Big Idea

— _DAY 15_ —

My Big Idea

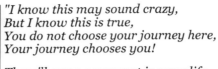

"I know this may sound crazy,
But I know this is true,
You do not choose your journey here,
Your journey chooses you!

There'll come a moment in your life
When you are forced to choose,
*To wake up to your **special gift***
Or keep your life on snooze."

*"We are each born with a special gift that we alone were meant to bring into the world. Your gift is precious and desperately needed. **What is yours?**"*

Hal Price is an Inspirational Speaker, #1 Int'l Best-Selling, Award-Winning Author and a Master Storyteller. His passion is to help awaken children/parents to the power of their HEROIC HEART™.   HeroicHeart.org

My Big Idea

— _DAY 16_ —

My Big Idea

— DAY 17 —

*"As life is full of so many highs and lows that may bring joy and pain, **REALLY** living requires us to look within our own hearts for the truths that stop us from authentically living and then trust and love what's there with compassion. Since the Heart has eyes and ears of its own, we are truly our **OWN** visionaries when we listen to the voice within and speak our truths with power and passion."*

Susan L. Dascenzi, MSW, LCSW is an Emotion/Vision Coach, Licensed Therapist, International Best-Selling Author, and Speaker specializing in teaching women how to emotionally be free.   SusanDascenzi.com

My Big Idea

— _DAY 17_ —

My Big Idea

— *DAY 18* —

"Wellness is more than health, diet and exercise. It's also pleasure, joy, laughing and playing. It is what you believe, how you cope, your spiritual relationship; what makes you shine. The missing link to wellness is the ability to connect to your true self.

Wellness is about balance. Extreme focus on any one thing is not balance. Being aware of who you are at your core is your compass for a well and balanced life."

Lisa Meisels is an author, speaker, coach and the "Reconnection Catalyst" helping women reconnect with their true self, become healthier, feel alive and live an inspired life. Femanna.com

My Big Idea

— _DAY 18_ —

My Big Idea

— DAY 19 —

*"Crafting a compelling storyline, vivid characters and the narrator's voice in a romantic yet suspenseful setting is challenging. Ideas, details and dialogue flow without warning from the subconscious into the conscious mind at awkward times: on the freeway, in the shower, waiting in line, at dinner, or when doing a task. Tucked away in the imagination, these gems trickle out when you're **not trying** to write. Plan for how **you will** capture this precious booty."*

Linda S. Gunther is the author of three romantic thrillers available on Amazon and for Kindle: *Ten Steps From The Hotel Inglaterra, Endangered Witness* and *Lost In The Wake*. LindaSGunther.com

My Big Idea

— _DAY 19_ —

My Big Idea

*"You come to a point when you need to change, see things differently and take control of your life. This single act will allow you to grow, develop, create, innovate, learn, adapt and be flexible. It starts with your own decision and is the **transformational change** that will take you to new and different levels of performance. You become the **'change factor'** in your life. No one else will. No one else can."*

Luis Vicente Garcia is a business performance and entrepreneurial coach, international speaker, best-selling author and radio host. <u>LuisVicenteGarcia.com</u>

My Big Idea

_____
_____
_____
_____
_____
_____
_____
_____
_____
_____
_____
_____
_____
_____
_____
_____
_____
_____
_____
_____

— _DAY 20_ —

My Big Idea

_____
_____
_____
_____
_____
_____
_____
_____
_____
_____
_____
_____
_____
_____
_____
_____
_____
_____
_____
_____
_____
_____
_____
_____
_____
_____
_____
_____
_____
_____

— *DAY 21* —

"'The Big Picture View of You' ~ Whenever life gets challenging, expanding your view to see the larger picture reveals what's going wrong and right. Wider perspectives make problems seem smaller, while positive focus navigates you past obstacles and onto a higher road. Your big picture view is your 'highway' route to getting help, choosing roads of action, and helping others down the road. Therefore, life's bumps and curves can become your joy ride to clarity and living your higher purpose!"

Bonnie Gordon Patterino is a #1 Int'l Best-Selling Author, Speaker and Life Purpose Coach. She's helped thousands with her GPS Your Path™ life transformation methods.
GPSYourPath.com

My Big Idea

— _DAY 21_ —

My Big Idea

*"When praying for healing, remember the most well-known prayer in the Bible is **The Lord's Prayer**. Prayers for healing should always include 'Not my will, Lord, but yours be done.' This can be the hardest line to say, especially when you have a desperate healing need. Try to pray without fear and being anxious. This is difficult, but ask God to increase your faith and to give you peace through this time of trial."*

Rev. Rhonda D. Branch is a #1 Int'l best-selling author, speaker, advocate of abused children/domestic violence survivors, nonprofit expert and Talk Show Host of "Keeping It Real! With Rev. Rhonda!" AJourney2Healing.org

My Big Idea

_____
_____
_____
_____
_____
_____
_____
_____
_____
_____
_____
_____
_____
_____
_____
_____
_____

— <u>DAY 22</u>—

My Big Idea

"We are all capable of living a life we love - we just need to know how! The secret is defining and implementing your life's purpose, aligning it with your goals and your passions to create a clear vision of your journey. Determine what values and beliefs you want guiding your goals. Life is meant to be filled with abundance and joy. Stop living your fears, and start living your dreams. LIVE LIFE ON PURPOSE!"

Jim White, Ph.D. is the CEO and Founder of JL White International and the best-selling author of *What's My Purpose? A Journey of Personal and Professional Growth.* WhatsMyPurpose.com

My Big Idea

_____

_____

_____

_____

_____

_____

_____

_____

_____

_____

_____

_____

_____

_____

_____

_____

_____

_____

_____

_____

_____

_____

— _DAY 23_—

My Big Idea

— DAY 24 —

"Each of us has a special brilliance and a unique set of experiences! Outside of speaking, coaching, books or business-as-usual, when was the last time you did something free while feeling passionate about the recipient? Saying YES to helping someone else with your gifts will change lives – YOURS and THEIRS! I found a way to help nonprofit organizations using my interview skills to co-create videos so they thrive while assisting others. Where can you use your brilliance and talents today?"

Debbi Dachinger is a Media Personality, a successful motivational speaker and runs the *Radio Mastery Training* for entrepreneurs, speakers and authors ready to be superb while on air. DebbiDachinger.com

My Big Idea

— _DAY 24_ —

My Big Idea

— _DAY 25_ —

"Words of Wisdom from my Mom ~ She raised 5 children, made many sacrifices, was disciplined, had ethics and values and sold door-to-door beauty and household products every day. At the same time, she created a vision in our minds for a much better, faster and smarter way of making a living. This inspiration has taken me to levels of success that I couldn't imagine back then. Mom always told us, 'Find, Develop, ENJOY and SHARE your God-Given Gifts!'"

Leticia Fuerte, Author of eCourses and with complimentary meditations: *The Self-Love Diet* and <u>GodsPlanisMyplan.com</u>. Designed for emotional and energy healing for Personal Transformation at all levels.

My Big Idea

My Big Idea

— *DAY 26* —

"This day is the best day of the rest of your life. Nourish it!

Begin with an attitude of gratitude. Give thanks for everything.

Perform 3-12-minute meditation. Inhale deeply through nose; exhale slowly through mouth, releasing all thoughts.

Exercise. Your body and mind will reward you.

Focus on three most important items on to-do list. The remainder can wait.

Focus, smile, but step outside once an hour, allowing the sun to warm your closed eyelids."

Rose Scott's deep passion for body/mind connection is reflected in her fitness training, coaching, award-winning speeches and writing. 559-797-1593

My Big Idea

_____

_____

_____

_____

_____

_____

_____

_____

_____

_____

_____

_____

_____

_____

_____

_____

_____

— _DAY 26_—

My Big Idea

'"Treat others, as you would most want to be treated.' This Golden Rule is found in most beliefs and hearts, even to make friends of enemies.

Seek daily God's Holy Spirit within, as well as without, for Love to be!"

Betty C. Dudney is an Author and an Activist for Peace Vigils, Civil Rights, Farm Workers Unions and Co-Founder of WorldWideHumanRights.org and the non-profit Golden Rule Family. Equality4Peace.org

My Big Idea

_____

_____

_____

_____

_____

_____

_____

_____

_____

_____

_____

_____

_____

_____

_____

_____

_____

_____

_____

— *DAY 27*—

My Big Idea

— *DAY 28* —

*"Adults should live by the 'Four Cs' — **C**ultivating **C**hildren **C**reating **C**onfidence. Always Act as a role model. Children invariably imitate adult behavior - good and bad. If they see you cussing, they will cuss. If they see you praying, they will pray. If they see you helping others, they will help. Abused children are at a higher risk of being in abusive relationships as adults as well as being abusers of others without adequate personal therapy."*

Ingrid Harris Edwards is a business professional, wife, mother of 5 (3 are adopted) and grandmother. Ingrid and Fred foster leveled and high-risk children.
IngrdEdwards@gmail.com

My Big Idea

— _DAY 28_—

My Big Idea

— DAY 29 —

"Life after infidelity can be very challenging. It is a very traumatic experience that will change your life. Instead of allowing it to keep you down, use it as a stepping stone and come out stronger. Don't allow your spouse's betrayal to define who you are. Put your-self first and figure out the best way for You to move forward with your life and be the empowered woman God has made you to be."

Tameka Calloway, Founder and Speaker of "Life After Infidelity" by Calloway's Coaching, is an expert Infidelity Recovery Specialist. <u>CallowaysCoaching.com</u>

My Big Idea

— *DAY 29* —

My Big Idea

"Henry David Thoreau said, 'What lies behind us and what lies before us are small matters – compared to what lies within us.'

Human beings are multi-dimensional beings. Meeting people, including our children, in the way they relate or in the manner in which they learn, whether it be on a Physical, Mental, Emotional or Spiritual Level, allows us an opportunity to get a glimpse of that inner light that we are all born with."

Mary M. Ernsberger, M.Sc., M.Ed., is a Clinical Herbalist, Hypnotherapist, ADHD Coach, author of *un-Broken Children: Removing Labels Restoring Health & Wellness* and Founder/Owner of NaturesSimpleRemedies.com

My Big Idea

— _DAY 30_—

My Big Idea

"Still playing by the rules? ~ When you think about creating your life, what do you imagine? Words or images from your parents or your third grade teacher? If so, then you're still playing by their rules - the conscious and unconscious messages you've used to create your life. This could be why you feel stuck, anxious, depressed, or just not yourself. To create a life you love, dig deeper within yourself to break free, and then, create your own transformational rules."

Licensed psychologist and consultant, **Edna Brinkley, PhD.** specializes in helping stressed out women create more peaceful, happier, and intentional lives.   BrinkleyCenter.com

My Big Idea

_____
_____
_____
_____
_____
_____
_____
_____
_____
_____
_____
_____
_____
_____
_____
_____
_____

— _DAY 31_—

My Big Idea

— *DAY 32*—

'"Live life as if everything is rigged in your favour.' ~ Rumi

A favourite quote by a favourite poet!! It's the belief that the universe is on our side, that all is well, and no matter what may be happening, it is for our ultimate good. In 'catastrophic' moments, I have consoled myself through tears, through gut-wrenching sorrow, through a crushed heart by repeating 'this TOO is serving me', and things work out because life is rigged in my favour."

Fariha Shah is a Philosopher, Author, Radio Personality, Cognitive and Political Scientist, Mother of 6 Astounding Individuals and Founder/Executive Coach of The Passion Practitioner. FarihaShah.com

My Big Idea

— _DAY 32_—

My Big Idea

"The key to success begins with a positive mindset. Through my own success in education, my career, and the work I have provided to others, I have discovered that a person's mindset strongly contributes to their own success. As an entrepreneur, you not only need to have a winning business idea. But you also need to think positively about the success of your business and be passionate to help your clients achieve their maximum results."

Dr. Kimberli Law, Best-Selling Author, Certified Coach and Educator, Founder of CTC for Women, where entrepreneurs learn mindset strategies to increase revenue to their business. CTCforWomen.com

My Big Idea

— _DAY_ 33—

My Big Idea

"Whether it's a relationship issue, starting a new career/business, or relocating to a new environment, people can become consumed with the 'what if I fail' mindset. Every day in my profession I encounter the 'play it safe' people—caused by an inner stifling fear of rejection.

*If you want things in life to **REALLY** change for the better, you need to get out of the passenger seat, puke in the bucket, and change your story **now**!"*

Nancy Bagley, CRMC, MS, Creator of "Change Your Story" signature series, LIFE Leadership Development Coach, Founder of Harvard Solutions & Co., personal/professional products and services.   HarvardSolutionsCo.com

My Big Idea

— *DAY 34* —

My Big Idea

— DAY 35 —

"One of the most powerful ways to transform your money story is through journaling. Especially if the topic brings up feelings of discomfort. The most common negative emotions around money are shame and guilt. Do you need to forgive yourself for past money mistakes? Then pull out your journal and write. A small dose of compassion will go a long way toward releasing regrets of the past, and transforming your money story into one of financial empowerment."

Patti Fagan, Certified Money, Business & Life Coach, Retired Financial Advisor, Best-Selling Author, Expert on Women, Money & Retirement. PattiFagan.com

My Big Idea

My Big Idea

"Learning about mental illness benefits everyone. Mental illnesses are still feared and misunderstood by people. Mental health education helps to reduce fear when people learn how to identify signs, signals and risk factors. Increasing our knowledge about mental health is vital in defeating prejudice, stigma, and discrimination towards individuals who suffer. 90% of people with mental illness who receive treatment are on the path to recovery."

Diana Kendros Makeig, Best-Selling Author, Life Coach, Mental Health First Aid Certified, Executive Director of Hope for Life organization, increasing mental health awareness and suicide prevention.   HopeForLifeMentalHealth.org

My Big Idea

— *DAY 36*—

My Big Idea

— DAY 37—

"Wisdom comes with age, from the lessons we learn, from the mistakes we make in life. When we learn to listen to our inner guidance, we grow as human beings. We seem to live in a world that puts such importance on youth. We spend so much time trying to turn back the clock and most of us don't look forward to aging. I love embracing age and gaining wisdom through this thing called life."

Devin DeVasquez is an actress, a producer of the Emmy-Winning *The Bay-The Series*, and co-owner of DevRonn Enterprises with husband Ronn Moss. DevRonn.com

My Big Idea

— _DAY 37_—

My Big Idea

— _DAY 38_—

"Everyone is gifted with a piece of the puzzle. Everyone and everything on this planet (and in the Universe) has an important contribution to make. We get stuck on the idea that we have to be 'doing' something. An experience is just an experience - until we apply our perspective. Our thoughts are responsible for our perception of reality. You shape reality with the power of your creativity. Bring your own unique color to the world."

Angel Fullerton is an International Best-selling Author, Intuitive Life Coach, Nonprofit Outreach and Development Coordinator, soulofthedragonfly.com Founder - Illuminating Lives to Overcome Darkness.

My Big Idea

— *DAY 38* —

My Big Idea

— DAY 39 —

"Breathe, shoulders down, relax and smile! Stress is part of our biology, a physical reaction and it is a survival mechanism. Don't try to fight it, instead get to know your own reactions, your own patterns and deal with them. Pause now and then and take a deep breath. That is the only way you can become really stress free and live the good life you dream about. Remember – only you can change your life!"

Annika Sörensen, MD, Author, International Speaker, Mentor, Seminars, Strategic Sessions and more. Helping Business Leaders feel less stress, get more done and create bigger success! <u>AskDrAnnika.com</u>

My Big Idea

— *DAY 39* —

My Big Idea

"Put chocolate in your pill box to fuel your soul throughout the rollercoaster of life's challenges. The pill box is a metaphor for your calendar. The chocolate represents whatever brings you pleasure. Our calendars get filled with must-do appointments and tasks. Strive to put at least one enjoyable activity of choice in your calendar each week. By dosing yourself regularly with joy, you will sustain your energy to accomplish your goals and meet your responsibilities."

A. Michael Bloom, MA, MS, is a Best-Selling Author, Coach, Speaker, and Caregiving Without Regret™ Expert. Revitalizing the careers of family and professional caregivers at CaregivingWithoutRegret.com.

My Big Idea

— _DAY 40_—

My Big Idea

"I've been helping people plan their Celebration of Life Event and writing some basic information for their obituary since 1976. When you do this, you will feel a sense of completing an important task and will be appreciated by your family and friends as one gigantic gift. A wonderful way to begin this process is to complete your bucket list ASAP. One sentence in my obituary will read, 'George and his wife, Linda completed their bucket list in 2013.'"

Rev. George McLaird has been a Presbyterian Pastor for 48 years and is an author of 7 books covering engagement, marriage, divorce, spiritual living and dying. McLaird.com

My Big Idea

— _DAY 41_ —

My Big Idea

— DAY 42—

"Reset to Success ~ In order to have success in your life, the first step is to reveal where you are. The second step is to determine what you want to achieve. Then you need to create a plan to accomplish that followed by taking action and implementing your plan. Finally you need to keep track of your progress and celebrate your wins. By consistently following this formula, you will experience the success you seek in your life."

Daniel Hanzelka is a Business Success Coach, Reset Warrior and Resetpreneur. He is an author and co-founder of The RESET Formula; a formula for creating the success you desire. ResetYourMoney.com

My Big Idea

— _DAY 42_—

My Big Idea

"Writing can be such a solitary endeavour, in reality. However, if I count all the ongoing conversations with the Committee inside my head, I suppose it does become rather a self-collaborative effort. And finding the voice that exactly fits the client I'm writing for can sometimes be a challenge, so it's a good thing I often have so many to choose from. I really can't think of a more enjoyable way to spend our time."

Lily-Ann MacDonald is an author/editor with her company, Write-Rightly Full Service Editing and Writing Agency, a book shepherd, and award-winning writer/editor with StarPoint Media Group.   Write-Rightly.com

My Big Idea

— _DAY 43_ —

My Big Idea

"Live the language of your heart! Involve and engage yourself only in the things that you love and leave out those that don't inspire you. You will get more clients that appreciate your authenticity and your Journey to the top will be fantastic. You feel strong; you feel unlimited and alive. Your creativity increases. Your personal presence just lights up. You will be amazed how caring will bring the connections you need to succeed."

Juracy Johnson, Best-Selling Author, Speaker and Master Coach in Latin America for Women who want to increase their Personal and Professional Presence.   JuracyJohnson.com

My Big Idea

— *DAY 44* —

My Big Idea

"Too many businesses think of their customers as just a number. Don't fall into that trap. Instead, find creative and meaningful ways to create value for your clients and prospects, and you will generate an impact, build rapport, and ultimately be rewarded.

An easy yet powerful way to create value is to generate a smile or laugh. Magic tricks and visual gags tied to your message are great for this. Brighten somebody's day today!"

Joe Libby, Entertainer, Speaker, Author from San Antonio, TX; Founder of "Causes for Laughter" FUN-d Rai$ing Program, raising no-risk money and awareness for schools, churches and nonprofits.   JoeLibby.net

(Photo by Jacklen Taylor of Outlaw Photography.)

My Big Idea

— *DAY 45* —

My Big Idea

— DAY 46—

"Gone are the days of chasing friends and family to try your product or service. Attraction Marketing works and works well because it emanates from a foundation of service. We serve others with authenticity and genuine desire to help. Do this and the world will come to you.

Enlightened and empowered home business entrepreneurs use Attraction Marketing and S.M.A.R.T. Goals to turn their passions into success. Be enlightened, be authentic, be empowered, and Be Great!"

Yvette Brisco, M.S., Author, Speaker, Empowerment Coach, Attraction Marketing Coach, Wellness Coach, S.M.A.R.T. Goals Specialist and MMA Official. YvetteBrisco.com

My Big Idea

_____
_____
_____
_____
_____
_____
_____
_____
_____
_____
_____
_____
_____
_____
_____
_____
_____

— *DAY 46*—

My Big Idea

— DAY 47—

"People think self-discipline comes easily to me because I was an athlete. Between ages 7 and 18, I was up at 4am every morning to swim laps, play tennis and compete at fairly high levels in both sports.

That, however, was an imposed discipline by my parents to fulfill their dreams for me; this was not self-discipline nor was it my dream.

I now have big dreams for myself: an opportunity to learn real self-discipline."

Kaylan Daane is an International Best-Selling Author in the anthology, *Pebbles In the Pond-Wave Three*. She is now working on her autobiography and several fiction books. KaylanDaane.com

My Big Idea

— _DAY 47_ —

My Big Idea

"Many people ask, 'What is my purpose? What are my gifts?' Instead of asking, CHOOSE! Choose any gift you desire.

To ask 'What are my gifts?' suggests that someone other than YOU gets to choose. When in truth, you can have any gift you choose if you only choose it, nurture it, develop it, and then it is yours. So choose!"

Dr. Lisa Turner, Founder of Psycademy, is a master spiritual trainer specializing in the release of emotional and spiritual pain, allowing people to access higher states of consciousness.   Psycademy.co.uk

My Big Idea

— <u>DAY 48</u>—

My Big Idea

"I want every person to have the freedom to choose their experience of life. Your past is controlling your choices from fear, concern, doubt, survival. It is your time NOW to set yourself free, to create, live abundantly, be who you are meant to be. Learn the secrets that will give you the keys to attracting your new life to you NOW. Time to stop daydreaming and start living your dreams!"

Heather Szasz is the Founder of Wealthy MindSet Mentor. Reprogram your mindset, take action NOW!
WealthyMindSetMentor.com

My Big Idea

— _DAY 49_—

My Big Idea

— *DAY 50*—

"Often we start doing something because we act on a feeling from the heart. As time goes on, we can lose connection with our heart and start acting from our head.

Pause! ~ Stop! ~ Breathe! ~ Repeat!

Take a moment to become aware of what you are doing and why.

Reconnect with your heart and let your feelings, thoughts and actions flow from there.

Notice the difference between head and heart; then choose where you start everything from."

Naomi Martell-Bundock is a wellbeing and stress management expert for Neom Organics, BootsWebMD and BBC Radio who can help you "Take back control of your life."
CoreSense.co.uk

My Big Idea

— *DAY 50* —

My Big Idea

— DAY 51 —

"What's Stopping Your Big Idea? Often the biggest barrier to making your Big Idea a reality is not finding funding or the right people; it's your own internal 'fear fence.'

When a fear fence pops up, it's exasperating as it stops you AND you can see through to the other side. While each fence is unique, the first step to get over any fear fence is to consciously take slow, deep breaths to calm your fear response."

Sharon Sayler, **MBA, PCC**, is a behavioral communications expert dedicated to teaching professionals how to get the results they want using critical influence, verbal and nonverbal skills. SharonSayler.com

My Big Idea

— _DAY 51_—

My Big Idea

"Beyond being healthy and strong our-selves, the next best strategy for helping those on the autism spectrum is to understand the difference between our social nature and the non-social orientation of the person with autism. That perspective allows us to develop a relationship that fully honors and serves both parties. Armed with that understanding plus deep self-knowledge and persistent self-care, we hold the keys to a successful relationship with a person with autism."

Jeanne Beard is a graduate of Northwestern University, Speaker, Coach, Author of *Autism & The Rest of Us* and Founder of the National Autism Academy.
NationalAutismAcademy.com

My Big Idea

— _DAY 52_—

My Big Idea

*"Want to develop your confidence? Step outside your comfort zone, challenge yourself regularly and realize that every experience - even when it feels like failure - is an opportunity to learn. Don't wait to be smarter, slimmer or fitter. Get on stage and give a talk to 300 people, run a marathon, do things that scare you; you will survive! The more you do them, the more confidence you will gain. Remember Confidence Comes **AFTER** the Act, not before!"*

Jenny Garrett is an award-winning Executive Coach, TEDx Speaker, Trainer and Author of *Rocking Your Role*, the guide to success for female breadwinners. JennyGarrett.Global

My Big Idea

— *DAY 53* —

My Big Idea

"Take a close look at the world around. Look deeper. Stop still and listen to your heart.

When making hard choices, be still and quiet to hear the murmured wisdom of your heart. It will surely guide you to the path that brings you the greatest joy.

When you sit in stillness and look deeper at the world around you, hidden opportunities come to view. Let your heart and quiet mind gently guide you."

Linda Emslie, a Transformation and Wellbeing Specialist, has helped hundreds of people in her local community to change the way they think, move and feel.   Lovlali.com

My Big Idea

— *DAY 54*—

My Big Idea

"'Everything affects everything else!'

*When you seek peak performance, you will do well to remember that everything you do either slows down or propels you toward your goal of excellence. Careful application of **the right stuff, in the right amount, at the right time**™ minimizes effort and maximizes results.*

On the road to your desired destination, pay attention to this mantra and you will increase your achievement, accomplishment, personal satisfaction, and it will be FUN!"

Raymond Perras (Peak Performance Coach), Int'l best-selling author, leadership development expert, creator of the Life Mastery Program™ for individuals seeking peak performance as a way of life.   coachrpp@gmail.com

My Big Idea

— *DAY 55* —

My Big Idea

"Networking success happens when you are interested in others as people, not just for what they can do for you, but for who they are. The more you learn about others, the stronger and more interconnected your relationships will become. Think "How can I help them?"

Ask: **How can I help you grow your business?**

How can I make you a hero to your clients?

Who do you need connection to?

Then Listen. Listen. Listen."

Susanne Romo, LUTCF, CFP is an Int'l Best-Selling Co-Author and is finishing her own book *Synergy Networking™: The Marketing Road Less Travelled.*
susanneromo@yahoo.com

My Big Idea

_____
_____
_____
_____
_____
_____
_____
_____
_____
_____
_____
_____
_____
_____
_____
_____
_____
_____

— _DAY 56_—

My Big Idea

*"If you have people or anything hindering your goal to succeed, you need to understand who and why and then **discover** methods to 'stack the deck' in your favor to live a thriving **lifestyle**. Random activity leads to random results. Your desired results will require a map of specific steps and tools for you to maximize your greatness within. By using specific strategies, you can rethink, redefine, reinvent, rekindle, and reclaim your 'Full Effect' lifestyle."*

Bernadette C. Broughton is a Certified Results Coach, President of LifeStyle DeSign, Founder of "Full Effect" Vision Board Workshops, and Self Mastery Expert ~ Transforming Passion into Excellence. BernadetteBroughtonsResources.com

My Big Idea

— *DAY 57*—

My Big Idea

"The Beach Boys sang about "Good Vibrations" and the reference was not lost on the listener. Upon beginning a new project, consider what vibrations are being created. Stress and frustration are not hallmarks of good vibrations.

Successful entrepreneurs mind their vibrations at all stages of their endeavors. Moments of gratitude and visualization set the stage for good vibrations. When choosing one product or service over another, people chose the one with the best vibrations. Vibe up!"

Julie Stamper is an international best-selling author in the anthology, *Pebbles in the Pond Wave Four*. She is a mixed-media artist and proprietor of Angel House Retreat. AngelHouseRetreat.com

My Big Idea

— DAY 58 —

My Big Idea

"We were made to create. As infinite beings on this three-dimensional reality, our highest calling is to first love. And out of pure unconditional love comes creation. The Creator gave the mandate to go forth and multiple -to create, recreate and procreate. To us, creation is easy, is natural, the essence of life, and we get to practice it every day. With love, you can choose and create the life and the world you want."

Andrew Gowan is a leading Naturopath, Bowen® Therapist, nutritionist, researcher, musician, quantum jumper, author, and father of seven talented children and he lives creatively. AndrewGowan.com

My Big Idea

— *DAY 59* —

My Big Idea

"Healthy body relies on healthy mind, healthy body brings healthy mind. All harmony starts from inner peace! Meditation, reflection and breathing create harmony, peace and space. Movement and rhythm create energy.

Nurturing our body and mind brings new life. Walking, meditation and introspection are essential for a healthy mind and healthy body. Healthy food nurtures our body and soul. Nature, grace and peace are three of lives treasures."

Being a thought leader of natural healing for three decades, **Quli Zhou** has been dedicating herself to helping live their life purpose through health and vitality. myeternalhealth.com

My Big Idea

— <u>DAY 60</u>—

My Big Idea

"Love is always the answer — and it starts with loving your SELF. Compassionate Communication fosters peace, love and joy. You become more loving, compassionate, kind, sorry, and grateful. Your attention, affection, acceptance, and appreciation model gratitude for your whole family to emulate. No matter how old your children are — or how long it's been since you offended your partner (or your ex) — a sincere 'I'm sorry' is a priceless gift you can bestow at any time."

Linda Kroll is a therapist, mediator, attorney, and author of the Amazon best-seller, *Compassionate Mediation® for Relationships at a Crossroad: Add Passion to Your Marriage or Compassion to Your Divorce.*   LindaKroll.com

My Big Idea

— DAY 61—

My Big Idea

"Thrive in our profoundly changing world by adopting the essential skill of 'learning, unlearning and relearning' new thoughts, ideas and ways of living. You'll live life more fully. More skilled, open and expanded, you're now more resilient and adaptable to change. You become like a palm tree. In a tsunami, it can be stretched, swayed and ruffled to its core. Yet, it always bounces back standing strong amidst a flattened terrain. Empowering your-self equals more happiness!"

Bernadette Dimitrov, aka Australia's 1st official Mrs. Claus, is an International Best-Selling Author, Head Trainer and Founder of SantaClausPeaceSchool.com and Happiness & Peace Ambassador.

My Big Idea

— <u>DAY 62</u>—

My Big Idea

— DAY 63—

"Why make unwanted things your business? If you aspire to attract your true and pure desires, you need the genius of intention and imagination. It's a way of giving yourself permission to honor the Goddess within – the Spirit who reveals unseen treasures of your heart. Follow this UNKNOWN path with a KNOWING that you're guided. Only then can you develop 'eyes' that see through the matrix of rules and let your magic flow..."

Therra Weinberg, Best-Selling Author, Speaker, Artist, founder of Sakkacise - a transformational coaching program equipping you with Afrobeat-fitness, spiritual and holistic tools to manifest a life of total wellbeing!   Sakkacise.com

My Big Idea

— _DAY 63_—

My Big Idea

— $\mathcal{DAY}$ 64—

"I believe that passion and purpose in what we do and who we be is paramount to a happy and healthy career and life. If we follow this path, the wealth is sure to follow. Finding balance in life is a continuous journey. Make the journey fun by knowing that every step builds and strengthens our soul. Even darkness helps us appreciate the light and struggle makes success sublime. Follow your path; embrace the journey!"

Phil Ross is the Best-Selling Author of *Soul Destiny Discovery, Soul Destiny The Master Key, Creative Thoughts* and producer of The Master Key Program by Soul Destiny. Phil@MasteryDevelopmentGroup.com

My Big Idea

— *DAY 64* —

My Big Idea

— DAY 65—

"Being responsible and at cause for your world is a tough gig and the most rewarding, empowered and calming place to be. Loving who you are and what you do is a choice that we make every second of every day. Imagine a universe of empowered and loving people. It all starts with you. What can you do TODAY that will allow you to be more in love with you, responsible for your world and empowered?"

Lynda Dyer is a 7-time International Best-Selling Author, Coach and Master NLP Trainer. Lynda is passionate about assisting people to realize their own magnificence and share it. MindPowerGlobal.com.au

My Big Idea

— *DAY 65*—

My Big Idea

— DAY 66 —

"Fear of failure is a limiting belief. Feeling "stuck" often occurs and is natural. Express your fears. It's time for you to process what's happened and reflect on your life; for you to acknowledge the past; get grounded and centered in the present and plan for the future. This is the time for setting goals to move toward the life you want.

*Your goals need to be SMART: **S**pecific, **M**easurable, **A**chievable, **R**ealistic, and **T**ime-Dependent."*

Marcia Merrill is a Business and Life Coach who guides women entrepreneurs to success! Sign up for a complimentary Live w/ Passion Session at MidlifeTransitionCoaching.com

My Big Idea

_____
_____
_____
_____
_____
_____
_____
_____
_____
_____
_____
_____
_____
_____
_____
_____
_____
_____
_____

— _DAY 66_—

My Big Idea

— _DAY 67_—

*"Dreams are majestic. They're boundless. However, if you wish to achieve them, they must be tempered with goals and plans. Take the time to sift through what you **want** to accomplish then write your plans in as much detail as possible. There is something powerful, even magical, about putting these thoughts into written form. Review your plans regularly and make adjustments as needed. Your dreams will manifest with your heart's work."*

Bonnie L. Boucek is a Best-Selling Author, Creative Visionary, Fibromyalgia & Chronic Pain Life Coach, Educator, Reverend and Mother. BonnieBoucek.com

My Big Idea

— *DAY 67*—

My Big Idea

— DAY 68—

"What if we re-calibrated the grand expectations we place on ourselves, and instead made small changes we could implement right now? Sometimes we need to take a huge leap - but more often, we need to make just a one-degree shift to put ourselves on a different, happier, trajectory. Checking in with and then tweaking our posture or language can transform how we feel, think and act. What small shifts could you make today?"

Cath Grey assists those who are ready to break free from stress or stuckness in relationships, career, or life itself, to get the clarity and purpose they need to thrive.
MindfulCoast.com

My Big Idea

— _DAY 68_—

My Big Idea

— *DAY 69*—

"Choice takes courage. With choice we find new potential and purpose as a life of integrity and authenticity unfold to us. Release the conditioning and enter into the journey of finding balance. Take a leap of faith; partner with the universe. The road ahead leads to the greatest version of ourselves, and it's there we find our lives' deepest calling. Commit to live more fully into balance. You always have a choice, use it wisely."

Danielle Corenchuk is an Author, Speaker, Entrepreneur, Trainer, Founder of Your Moment in Life Coaching & Personal Development, Prolympian PTSD Coach, and Philanthropist. YourMomentInLife.com

My Big Idea

— *DAY 69*—

My Big Idea

— DAY 70—

"We first acquire vision by opening our eyes. As we grow, we see not only with the body's eyes, but through opening our hearts and minds. Opening up to what is truly before us and within us spurs our human development. Are we seeing what we want to see or what we need to see? Wisdom is recognizing both and feeling accordingly, yet perceptively targeting the truth to hasten growth in us all."

Anne Redelfs, MD, a retired psychiatrist and author of *The Awakening Storm,* now practices as a "listener" who helps people hear their souls' communications in ordinary life events. annethelistener.org

My Big Idea

— _DAY 70_—

My Big Idea

— DAY 71—

 *"Your Intuition is the greatest gift an author has. The intuition allows you to access parts of yourself that are unavailable when consciously trying to write. I do a short meditation before I begin any writing and move my consciousness into a state where I can readily ask my intuition for guidance, for input, for suggestions and for options. Then I listen. Marvelous ideas flow to me ... I am amazed ... and I write them all down."*

Dana E. Kellogg is an International Best-Selling Author, Speaker, Coach and Spiritual Director.
authordekellogg@gmail.com

My Big Idea

My Big Idea

"When enough people reach a place of deep surrender to Life while being willing to act out that surrender in the world, no matter what the risks, we activate the sacred masculine presence that can rise up out of the living cells of humanity and assume a global presence. At that time, this merging of his presence with her love can collapse the infinite wave of future possibilities into a path of global healing."

Alistair Smith is a visionary pioneer using his healing journey with cancer to bring insights into the plight of humanity and our global healing potential. awakenthesacredmasculine.com

My Big Idea

— _DAY 72_—

My Big Idea

"Trust in yourself at every turn. Whether it is business or personal, you must learn to trust your intuition. The moment you seek outside advice, you begin to question your own inbuilt guidance system; everything changes. The perspective of the advisor will be very different from the one you have. It is not necessarily better or worse but different and that variation must be factored in to any decision you make."

Kathie Holmes is a Best-Selling Author, Intuitive Mentor and Holistic Business Specialist supporting those in the fields of natural therapies/healing.   KathieHolmes.com

My Big Idea

— *DAY 73*—

My Big Idea

— *DAY 74* —

~ *The Success Blueprint* ~
1. *Find your passion.*
2. *Commit to your dreams.*
3. *Develop a clear plan of action and an attainment timeline.*
4. *Take action every day.*
5. *Maintain a positive attitude every day.*
6. *See obstacles and challenges as possibilities.*
7. *Concentrate on your strengths and values.*
8. *Come from your heart to help others.*
9. *Have a mastermind team or mentor support your journey.*
10. *Acknowledge and celebrate your successes along the way.*

Charlene Day is a Lifestyle and Leadership Coach, Mindset Breakthrough Expert, speaker, and author of 8 books with 3 being international bestsellers. CharleneDay.com

My Big Idea

My Big Idea

"We often tell ourselves that our pain is unique and no one can understand. Because we view our pain as unique, we often live with it for a very long time. The reality is that whether you are dealing with cancer, a breakup, bankruptcy, childhood trauma or abuse – the pain is the same. The sooner we recognize that, the sooner it stops having power in our life."

Robert Longley is a coach, consultant and entrepreneur. His inspirational poems have been used in movies, songs, and as memorials for police, fire and the military.
SacredPoems.com

My Big Idea

— DAY 75 —

My Big Idea

— DAY 76—

"Money and Spirituality are not mutually exclusive. You need money to live, and the more you make, the more you can give away. If you want to start generating money, make it your spiritual practice. Enjoy the money you make instead of hoarding it or killing yourself to make it. Rather than focusing on your own success, focus on making others successful. That creates a rising tide that lifts all boats, including your own!"

Jill Hendrickson, Best-Selling Author and Founder of Karmic Koaching, teaches people how to experience more success and abundance using ancient cause-and-effect karma principles. JillHendrickson.com   KarmicKoaching.com

My Big Idea

— _DAY 76_—

My Big Idea

— DAY 77—

"Writing and or journaling is the beginning to understanding who You are and what You are here to do. Through the tears and frustration that starts most journaling journeys, there is a roadmap being manifested with each word. A roadmap to bring You from the depths of uncertainty into the depths of a clearer vision in which You become the author and finisher of Your life. Reconnecting with Your Higher Self is worth the journal."

Natesha Renee is an author, the President & CEO of I Matter to Me: Affirming Mind, Body & Spirit balance, and a Life Coach specializing in sexuality and spirituality balance. imattertomembs@gmail.com

My Big Idea

_____
_____
_____
_____
_____
_____
_____
_____
_____
_____
_____
_____
_____
_____
_____
_____
_____
_____
_____

— *DAY 77*—

My Big Idea

"*If you choose only one thing for your evolution, choose timelessness. Choose to defy your mind's inclination to live in the past or the future, enslaving you to time. Choose to live where you actually are: HERE. NOW. Choose to fully invest in the eternal Now, where worrying naturally drops away, where there are no 'what-ifs,' and where your existence becomes infinite. Choose timelessness.*"

Janita van der Walt, LMHC, Psychotherapist, Life Coach, Author, Retreat Leader and Co-Founder of *AmanziLiving* and its signature program, *Living Like Water*. AmanziLiving.com

My Big Idea

My Big Idea

"Be the Best Version of Yourself ~ In order to exude confidence, poise, charm, appeal, and abundance, we must study what we wish to become. Lack of money or time should not deter our quest for self-improvement. Libraries are free and have both audio and downloadable books. Listen to an author while on your commute; read a book on your smartphone while on public transportation. Knowledge is power! Use it to become the best version of yourself."

Shirley Jusino, Int'l #1 Best-Selling Co-Author of *Ready, Aim, Thrive!*, Speaker, Life Coach, and a certified Law of Attraction Practitioner through Global Sciences Foundation. ShirleyJusino.com   ShirleyJusino@ymail.com

My Big Idea

— _DAY 79_—

My Big Idea

— *DAY 80*—

"Seeing the media images and hearing the TV commentators, it is easy to become fearful. Underneath fear is anger, bitterness and self-pity, which limits your choices and causes hatred and division. Take care of yourself. Start the day telling yourself, 'I will be strong and courageous. I'll be okay no matter what comes my way.' You will become more resilient and will impact others by your calmness."

Ruth Littler is a Trauma Resilience Counselor and Coach at Brilliant Living. BrilliantLiving.net.au

My Big Idea

My Big Idea

A Message From Shelter Animals

Love me *because no matter what the circumstances were that brought me here, I have a heart and soul like you, and I understand love.*

Love me *and don't pity me, because I don't understand pity. I might know fear, rejection, and cruelty, but I also know happiness and joy, and I just want a family to love.*

Love me *because I will love you back. Even if I'm scared and need lots of encouragement, I can learn to trust again.*

Make Adoption Your Option!

Wendy Rumrill has volunteered at the SPCA of NE NC since 2010. She is pictured with Hines, just one of the many animals available for adoption.   WendyRumrill.com

My Big Idea

My Big Idea

*"What if there was a **design** or **thinking** methodology that was so compelling that it could potentially solve any problem, whether at work or something personal? Our lives would change forever. When **Design Thinking** principles are applied to strategy, innovation or real-world challenges, the success rate for a solution improves dramatically. **Design Thinking** is a user-centered approach that brings together* technology feasibility, customer needs, *and* business viability *for a successful innovation, business or outcome."*

J. K. Chua, Best-Selling Author, Entrepreneur, Speaker, Coach/Mentor, Master Facilitator/Trainer of Design Thinking for Business Excellence to Thrive and Personal Success. jkchua@octoneon.com   JKCHUA.com

My Big Idea

_____

_____

_____

_____

_____

_____

_____

_____

_____

_____

_____

_____

_____

_____

_____

_____

_____

My Big Idea

"Do you fear the future? A record number of sage women have put their mid-life's desires on hold. Rather than dread that retirement may never come, or give up on your dreams reclaim your freedom and live a soulful life now!

You have an innate gift from your ancestors. Your character traits — your most valuable asset, by employing these free and easy to use eternal echoes you can start living your life fully today!"

Larry and Halette King-Meyer, Ph.D., are co-founders of The HeArt of Living Practical Wisdom System.
TheHeArtofLiving.com

My Big Idea

My Big Idea

"Love is the most worthless of all human emotions. The most misunderstood, incorrectly expressed, yet the most sought after. We are born with an unlimited supply that we guard selfishly most of our lives, afraid of its awesome power to either destroy us or heal us. It is too late in life that we learn that Love has absolutely no value until it is given away. Once it is freely given it sweetly returns tenfold."

D. Crystal Johnson is an Author, Speaker, Certified Life Coach, Intuitive Healer and Artist. Crystal has a spiritual commitment to helps others to become the best they can be. PassionateParadigm@cybertrails.com

My Big Idea

My Big Idea

— DAY 85—

"A transformational journey to creating an extraordinary life you love starts by embracing your unique story. There are so many amazing and unique stories out there waiting to be heard. Don't hold yourself anymore by not being visible to the world. It's about time you tell your story, take inspired actions, manifest more abundance, help and inspire more people! It's time to give the world the gift of your unique message!"

Kristine Pierce is a Best-Selling Author, Author Coach, Branding Strategist, Speaker, Founder of Inspired Action Publishing, Host of Write, Publish, Inspire! Podcast. KristinePierce.com

My Big Idea

—*DAY 85*—

My Big Idea

_____
_____
_____
_____
_____
_____
_____
_____
_____
_____
_____
_____
_____
_____
_____
_____
_____
_____
_____
_____
_____
_____
_____
_____
_____
_____
_____
_____
_____
_____
_____
_____
_____
_____

— DAY 86—

"Would You Like the Solution to Being an Inspired and Innovative Leader, without the Pressure that Usually Prevents You from Playing at the Top of Your Game? Innovative, creative Leaders have one thing in common...a Purpose that is bigger than their work, a Purpose that IGNITES their heart with a deeper Love. When you IGNITE your heart, you are a contribution to others and your work is a JOY!"

MichelJoy DelRe, Speaker, #1 Int'l Best-Selling Author, Business Consultant to over 5,000 CEOs and Entrepreneurs, Women's Leadership Coach in the Millionaire Mind Mastery 90-Day Game.   MillionaireMindMastery.com

My Big Idea

— *DAY 86* —

My Big Idea

— DAY 87—

"Think about the majestic perfection that is nature. Everything in nature is interdependent and cooperative. Everything has a cycle of birth, growth, death, and rebirth. Nature constantly adapts to changing conditions. Plants and animals do what they are designed to do without complaint or resistance. By paying attention to nature, you attune your body to the same flawless design and infinite supply of life force energy that unfolds year after year, right outside your window."

Amitra Grace, award-winning author of *Reclaiming Aphrodite - The Journey to Sexual Wholeness*, Certified Spiritual Sexual Educator, High Priestess, and founder of the *Dancing with Cancer*© paradigm. AmritaGrace.com

My Big Idea

— *DAY 87*—

My Big Idea

— *DAY 88*—

"DOLPHIN SECRETS: from a nonhuman intelligence.

1. Dolphins live without resistance, soaring through the ocean's vortices and currents; We breathe, enter the sea . . . float . . . relax . . . and surrender.

2. Dolphins, masters of relationship, are vibrantly interconnected to all; In the presence of dolphins, eye-to-eye, heart-to-heart, we become waves, timeless in the moment, one with the sea.

3. Immanent grace is the dolphin's art; Merge with pod consciousness, go in grace. "

As Dr. John Lilly's Research Director, **Roberta Goodman** initiated release of captive dolphins. Roberta now offers opportunities to release trauma and fear, encountering dolphins in the wild. WildDolphinSwimsHawaii.com

My Big Idea

— *DAY 88*—

My Big Idea

— *DAY 89*—

"There is more health information available than ever before yet there are more unhealthy and overweight people than ever before. Your health is your link to expansion and evolution. Being radiantly healthy allows you to express your True Self.

If you desire to live a victorious life then you require to have radiant health. Life force is the nectar of living and only with an abundance of it can you create the life of your dreams."

Rino Soriano known as the Conscious Health Alchemist, Author, Transformational Speaker, Founder of Body Brilliance Nutrition & Creator of Rino's Conscious Health Revolution. RinoSoriano.com

My Big Idea

My Big Idea

"Where there is a student there is a teacher. Where there is a teacher there is a student. We all teach and we all learn. It is the process of life. Know that the journey you take will always be worth the steps to get there. It all begins with one step. Take it and fill your life with courage, kindness and most of all 'Love.' Focus on love. It is the greatest of all."

Karen McCarthy, Inspirational Speaker and Author. Change your perception and change the world you live. She teaches you trust, love and to believe in you.
east710.wixsite.com/karenmccarthy

My Big Idea

— _DAY 90_—

My Big Idea

— *DAY 91* —

"Planning is bringing the future into the present where you can do something about it. Having a plan is crucial to focus where you want to go and how to achieve desired results. But it is not enough - 75% of plans fail. You must also have a systematic implementation process to monitor progress regularly, continuously improve, hold communications events, provide reminders to keep the plan in focus, hold yourself and others accountable for results."

Marcelene Anderson, MA, CMC, strategic planning and execution consultant and facilitator, author, and speaker. Managing director, Raven Strategic Consulting. www.RavenStrategic.com

My Big Idea

— _DAY 91_—

My Big Idea

"How will you make a difference in the world? One way is to bravely step into the light, and be a positive force through blogs, social media and books. Speak from your heart, as your authentic self, to enable others to realize they're not alone. Uplift, inspire, help, and heal. Your words may create positive changes and could even save a life! So be their voice, shine your light, and speak your truth: your way."

Fiona Louise is a writer, blogger, Natural Therapist, and Educational Psychology student after leaving corporate marketing management. Fiona has co-authored three international best-selling books.   Fiona-Louise.com

My Big Idea

— *DAY 92* —

My Big Idea

"You are special! You were born with a unique important life purpose to give to this planet in order to transform people's lives. If you are serious about awakening your talents, if you don't know your life purpose yet, or want to polish your talents and gift to contribute at greater levels to this planet, then you must take evolving your four bodies (Mental, Emotional, Physical, and Spiritual) to a greater level of growth."

Divina Caballo, Int'l Best-Selling Author of *Reawaken Your Authentic Self* and *The Butterfly Diet*, nutritionist, life purpose mentor, and Founder of Reawaken Your Authentic Self Academy. TheButterflyDiet.com
ReawakenYourAuthenticSelf.com

My Big Idea

— _DAY 93_—

My Big Idea

"Spirituality comes in many forms and no one should judge another before knowing the full story. Everyone's journey to her own truth is layered and we all choose our path based on the highest form of guidance available. As we grow, so does our guidance. We can use our intuition to connect with that guidance to overcome shame, guilt and even the judgement of others. Through that intuitive spiritual connection we can divine miracles."

Tricia Stewart Shiu, Best-Selling and 31 time Award-Winning Author, Speaker and Expert in Intuition in Business. TStewartShiu.com

My Big Idea

My Big Idea

*"When you want to do a U-turn in your work - or personal life and need help - use the 3-I's as the tools to do it. Set your **intention**, let **inspiration** and your **intuition** guide you on your path. Tune in and focus, this will help you to be open and in the flow, and wisdom will show you how to grow. Start living your dreams and inspire others to do the same."*

Jette Bilberg Lauritsen is an International Best-Selling Author, 3-I-coach and Poet. JetteBL.dk

My Big Idea

— <u>*DAY 95*</u>—

My Big Idea

— DAY 96—

"What if... everyone COMMITTED to the idea of setting our sights to LOVING--NO MATTER WHAT. That means, setting an INTENTION BEFOREHAND to SPEAK and ACT FROM THE HEART. Once the ego has thrown its first punch, then justifies the reaction--there's no turning back. If we change this antiquated response by acknowledging the value of kindness, calmness and consideration... there is a possibility of LOVING. WHAT WOULD IT TAKE FOR YOU TO COMMIT?"

Cher Slater Barlevi, M.A., Speaker, Retreats, Best-Selling Author of *Dog of God, The Novel, 365 Days of Angel Prayers, The Happy Divorce (If There's Such a Thing...Really?)* and others. CherSlaterBarlevi@yahoo.com, DogofGod.com

My Big Idea

My Big Idea

"When you start believing in yourself, you will find that ideas that seemed impossible before start to feel possible. The 'what ifs?' in life will turn into 'why nots?'; doubt and fear will no longer control your decisions. It takes courage and perseverance to keep asking yourself the big questions and to really listen for the answers. It may be the road less travelled, but it may also be your road to success."

Linda Valente, M.Ed, MFT, is passionate about coaching people to help them heal from destructive relationships and build new loving ones.   <u>LindaValenteCoaching.com</u>

My Big Idea

— _DAY 97_—

My Big Idea

"Do not let anyone decide for you what your success should look like. If someone does not understand the way you live, it is the limitation of their world, not yours. Your success and your life are the creation of your thoughts and your desires. Find a person who will support you in your journey in creating the life and the world you want and deserve. Think carefully, dream wisely, and live fearlessly."

Liina DeVries, Experienced and Heart-Centered Transformational Coach and Spirited Sage, working with clients who want to live their lives bravely, whole-heartedly and to their fullest potential. UACCTcoaching.com

My Big Idea

— _DAY 98_—

My Big Idea

— DAY 99—

"Hold onto your life. Grasp it with both hands. It is all you will ever have. Your family, friends, and relationships are vital to your well-being. Stay connected, involved, and strong. Become courageous. Someone needs you to be their hero. Speak only words of kindness. Be loving. Take care of your health. Stay informed by reading books and literature of all kinds. Be willing to give, listen, and forgive. Be prepared. Tomorrow may never come."

Lorraine Price, Best-Selling Author, Proofreader, Editor, and Book Reviewer, and Movie Critic for *When Magazine*.
linkedin.com/in/lorraineprice   Lprice9559@gmail.com
BestsellingAuthorsInternational.org/Lorraine-Price.html

My Big Idea

— _DAY 99_ —

My Big Idea

— *DAY 100*—

"Where There Is A Will There Is A Way ~ This is true to all who believe they can accomplish their goals. No matter how complicated or impossible a situation may appear to be, the individual who is determined to win the battle will find victory in overcoming the obstacles they encounter. Hard work and perseverance are the keys to obtaining that which you desire. You can do ALL things through Christ who strengthens you!"

Shirley Long is a mother, author, writer and songwriter. She has written romance novellas, short stories and how-to books.
TheRealisticTouch.wordpress.com

My Big Idea

— <u>DAY 100</u>—

My Big Idea

"You have two choices in life. Live the life you were born to live—OR—the life you have been conditioned to live. Live from conditioning and you will struggle between what you long to do and what you feel you have to do. There is another way.

Deep within your DNA is your soul's blueprint—your personal GPS—for living your best life. When you attune to and follow your blueprint, your struggle ends."

Nancy Monson, MA, MBA, CPCC, Founder of Everyday Spirituality: Living a Soul-Directed Life Every Day, Author, Speaker, Soul Purpose Advocate devoted to helping people live their soul's purpose. EverydaySpirituality.com

My Big Idea

— <u>*DAY 101*</u>—

My Big Idea

"Write From Life ~ A Journey About You ~ Experience the beauty of life in your own words.

Enjoy the freedom to express what is in your heart. Allow your heart to lead the way...

Now is the time to ignite the spark that fuels the flame for all your dreams and desires to come true.

Here's to a life well-lived and fully expressed."

Giselle Shapiro is a Visionary, Best-Selling Author, Midlife Women's Advocate, Speaker, Lifestyle Transformation Expert and Founder of LiteraryLaunch.com, an online global community for midlife women.

My Big Idea

— *DAY 102* —

My Big Idea

"This little light of mine, I'm going to let it shine! As a divine being of light, I am here to share my light through creative expressions of love.

For a season I hid my light under a bushel because I did not know its value, but I've come to know that sharing my light encourages others to share their light as well. You, too, have a light that you bring and you can choose to shine."

Veronica R. Lynch, Ph.D., is an Int'l Best-Selling Author, Director and Co-Founder of CreateWhole™ Wellness Services, providing tools for creating healthy life balance. CreateWhole.com   VeronicaRLynch.com

My Big Idea

— _DAY 103_—

My Big Idea

"We support our fellow man by matching their potential with their performance.

When potential shows up, we can then complete a task and it is considered an accomplishment.

When we get it right, it is considered an achievement.

As leaders, we create visionaries who may stumble over pebbles, but never over mountains.

We hold the authority to serve humanity in a very distinctive way, by revealing great ideas while fueling enthusiasm within others."

Dr. Janet Woods, Award-Winning Speaker, Philanthropist, Author and Futurist, and Founder of the Art of Life Institute. ArtofLifeInstitute.com

My Big Idea

— DAY 104 —

My Big Idea

— DAY 105—

"Your body is designed to heal itself when given what it needs. The basic needs of your body are nourishment for the mind, body and spirit. Nourish your body by feeding it healthy non-processed foods and participating in some form of movement on a regular basis. Nourish your mind and spirit by learning new things, having new experiences, learning to be still and seeking peace, joy and happiness."

Dr. Pam Middleton, Holistic Pediatrician, Int'l Best-Selling Author and Speaker. Dr. Pam has an Integrative Pediatrics practice in Newport Beach, CA.   myDrPam.com

My Big Idea

My Big Idea

"Creativity is thinking up new things.
Innovation is doing new things."
~Theodore Levitt

"Businesses need to have a clear sense of purpose, whilst adapting readily to unpredictable global business conditions. They need to have the courage to pursue and develop original creative ideas, and develop them at the right time. So that the idea can move markets, inspire colleagues and employees, and become a success, whilst moving forward and without endangering their business."

Melanie G. Robinson is a Best-Selling Author, Coach and entrepreneur, who lives with her family in the United Kingdom. facebook.com/melaniegrobinson

My Big Idea

— *DAY 106* —

My Big Idea

— *DAY 107*—

"In understanding how to change behavior, we all generally act based on the way we see the world, combined with our self-talk (what we say to ourselves), values and beliefs.

*When this isn't working to someone's potential, we have found change happens best starting from within, working on the self-talk and belief system, and developed values - listening for incongruities and passion opportunities, **sorting through, what someone really wants — then changing the self-talk to match.**"*

Rod Adkins is a Best-Selling Author, Speaker, Coach and Trainer. **"Change Starts From Within"**
Rod@ActionMind.com.au

My Big Idea

— *DAY 107*—

My Big Idea

— DAY 108—

"Whether we go through transformation willingly or not, we ALL will eventually be a butterfly. Solitude and inward reflection is the chrysalis providing shelter; the winter covering protecting the fragile seed as it discovers its own potential.

When we emerge, opening wings; when we blossom and share our beauty with the world, we are bound to experience profound gratitude for the frigid cold that shielded us from sunlight; for every bitter leaf we ate along the way."

"Presence" Tarika Brandt, D.D./Reverent, Performing Artist; Actor, Singer/Songwriter, Filmmaker, Counselor, Healing-Arts Practitioner, and Death-midwife performing worldwide concerts and as a volunteer at bedside for hospice. SacredSinging.LA

My Big Idea

— _DAY 108_—

My Big Idea

— DAY 109—

"We all face challenges during our quest for success, but it is how we interpret the challenge we are facing and how we react to it that makes us a failure or a success. What really helped me keep going and succeed was when I finally understood that success begins in the mind and in order to succeed with your life, first you must succeed with your mind. Success is all inside your mind."

Peter Nicado is an International motivational speaker and founder of The Winner's Mindset Academy. He is the author of the inspiring book, *The Winner's Mindset*.   PeterNicado.com

My Big Idea

— *DAY 109* —

My Big Idea

— *DAY 110*—

"It doesn't matter how talented or fabulous you are — if you don't eat right, slick combinations of sugar, chemicals and fat will topple you off your A-game. A body treated like a toxic dumping ground is a sure-fire way to derail your dreams by impeding productive flow!

Remember, big ideas are mobilized into physical action. Your relationship with food in cultivating a robust body becomes paramount. Consider your whole self a sacred temple — your diet and lifestyle the prayers."

Sarah Jane Michaels, "The Figure Queen" and "Love Magnet" - 8 time #1 Int'l Best-Selling Author, Weight Loss and Human Relationships Expert, and Speaker. La-Vitalita.com SarahJaneMichaels.com

My Big Idea

— _DAY 110_—

My Big Idea

"Everyone on earth has a vital purpose. Everything that happens to you, good and bad, is preparation for you to fulfill your divine destiny. Yes, you have one. Let past mistakes fade away. Let the future be a goal but not an obsessive one. Your greatest happiness will be found in the present moment. Notice the details and express daily gratitude. Master this for a well-loved, well-lived life."

Peggy Jaegly, Award-winning Author, Aspiring Author Coach, Founder of *Write Your Book* Tutoring, Speaker, and Professional & Therapeutic Harpist.
AuthorPeggyJaegly@aol.com

My Big Idea

— _DAY 111_—

My Big Idea

— DAY 112—

"What is the first thing you do when you awake? Is it early or late? Do you check your Facebook feeds or your emails first?

When it comes to developing a positive mindset, what we first consume (our first bites of information) at the start and at the end of each day creates an imprint in our mindset, moods and emotions.

Do you start and end with a positive focused winning mindset?"

Susana Tuya Sarmiento is an Int'l Inspirational Celebrity Speaker, TV Presenter, Journalist, Producer and #1 Best-Selling Author and highly sought after the media throughout Australia and New Zealand.   SusanaTuyaSarmiento.com

My Big Idea

— DAY 112—

My Big Idea

— *DAY 113*—

"Every Day Can Be A Great Day ~ Because YOU Choose! At night, say. . . .

'TODAY IS OVER' ~ *It allows you to recognize the closure of each day.*

'TOMORROW IS A NEW DAY' ~ *You are acknowledging your future has a clean slate.*

'IT WILL BE A GREAT DAY' ~ *Gifts you the opportunity of choice.*

'BECAUSE I CHOOSE' ~ *Is a place where you're in control.*

These sentences empower your greatness. ENJOY!"

Susan Shatzer is a 5-time #1 Int'l Best-Selling Author, single mom, Int'l facilitator, and has appeared multiple times on national TV.   SusanShatzer@gmail.com

My Big Idea

— _DAY 113_—

My Big Idea

— DAY 114—

"As most writers will have discovered by now, writing and editing your book is actually only the first step in becoming a successful author. You also need a detailed plan to promote it; and to do that effectively, you must raise your profile (brand) by marketing, public and media relations, and branding across all media outlets on and offline. Embrace your journey along the way and enjoy what it's making of you."

Beth McBlain, Author, Editor, Promoter, Publicist with strong client orientation by formulating and executing marketing, communications, branding, public/media relations strategies, event planning, collateral materials, researching and inspiring people. Beth.McBlain@gmail.com

My Big Idea

— *DAY 114*—

My Big Idea

— DAY 115—

"The past is like manure... when used properly it can be the fertilizer that transforms a dying crop into a field of food that sustains many lives. If ignored, it's just another mess waiting to be stepped in. Never be afraid of the past. Sure, it might stink, but it's fertile ground for a brighter future. How might your past lessons and experiences benefit yourself and others?"

Lori Anne Rising, Int'l Best-Selling Author, Nonfiction Author Coach specializing in influential nonfiction, Memoirist, and life-long learner with the intention of digging deeper and shining brighter every day.   LoriAnneRising.com

My Big Idea

— _DAY 115_—

My Big Idea

— DAY 116—

*"Your life is like a garden. You plant and tend it, **mindfully choosing** the types of seedlings, the seasons, the care bestowed upon it.*

*Is it hopeless...or precious and treasured? Is your garden more wasteland, filled with weeds and shadows, or is it **bursting** and **blooming** in sunlight, filling the air with fragrance and colour?*

You have only one garden. Finite time... infinite consequence and legacy.

Love your garden. What is within, manifests without."

Ursula Nieuwoudt from Namibia, SW Africa, Int'l Best-Selling Co-Author and Author of *Practical Conversations About Fitting In*. She is working on her next book about diamonds. UrsulaNieuwoudt.com

My Big Idea

— *DAY 116*—

My Big Idea

"Focus on your goals and your future... not where you were or where you are now. Hold the vision of your amazing future and what you are creating. Stand firm during challenging situations – you will come through this even stronger and more powerful than before.

Follow your heart and listen to your intuition as it will always guide to the right place. This will allow you to live a happy, fulfilled and abundant life."

Patricia LeBlanc, Best-Selling Author, CEO of Patricia LeBlanc International, Speaker, LOA Expert, Dream Maker and Empowering Female Entrepreneurs to get to the next level. LoaLifeCoaching.com

My Big Idea

— _DAY 117_—

My Big Idea

— DAY 118—

"If you do only one thing daily - express gratitude in the form of unconditional giving - your life will change in remarkable ways! I envision gratitude as the fountain of youth whereby all our innocence and humility pour forth into sparkling droplets of grace, and the wisdom contained therein has the power to keep us forever young. Like the fountain, our love is continuously being circulated from person to person and generation to generation."

Deborah Naone is an Author, Spiritual Life Coach and Mother of 2 whose mission in life is to participate in raising the consciousness of the planet.   DeborahNaone.com

My Big Idea

— _DAY 118_—

My Big Idea

— DAY 119—

"There is a yearning that comes from deep inside of you. That place in your innermost being that knows, more than your mind can comprehend, that you are more powerful than you are allowing yourself to be. That yearning, for something more, something different, even something better, is your spirit responding to the call of purpose – the call of greatness. I encourage you, Powerful One, when greatness calls, answer it with boldness."

Dr. Cherita Weatherspoon, Transformational Life Coach, Consultant, Author, Speaker and Founder of Powerhouse Coaching and Mission Critical Consulting. *Step into Your Power* at <u>CheritaWeatherspoon.com</u>

My Big Idea

My Big Idea

— DAY 120—

"As I wandered around Great Britain, I was often told I was brave to travel alone. I don't think I was brave. There were lots of places I wanted to see, and my dogs were happy to roam with me, so I grabbed some maps and we went.

Travelling solo can open doors you'd never know about otherwise. What are you waiting for? If you're ready to go, pack your bags and hit the road."

Gina Longo, a former airline Captain and author of the forthcoming book, *Britain Unleashed,* spent three years roaming Great Britain with her two German Shepherds. GinaM.Longo@yahoo.com

My Big Idea

My Big Idea

"Living Life in Five Hour Chunks, Tommy found that he was far more productive in twenty-five hours of focused work than many who put in a forty-hour plus work week: Five hours study or research; Five hours on focused work; Five hours with friends, family or community; Five hours deep sleep.

In between each of these five hour chunks, there's an hour to carry out the mundane routines of living — breakfast, lunch, dinner, toilet, shower, devotions."

Rod Hyatt is the author of *The Final Phoenix*, the fascinating account of Tommy, a strange young boy who yearned to be a millionaire. <u>FinalPhoenix.RodJHyatt.com</u>

My Big Idea

_____
_____
_____
_____
_____
_____
_____
_____
_____
_____
_____
_____
_____
_____
_____
_____
_____

— _DAY 121_ —

My Big Idea

— DAY 122—

"I dream of a world where everyone loves, encourages and respects each others' differences. Where compassion, courage and acceptance are the norm and judgment a thing of the past. I see this achieved by encouraging children, to be who they are, by teaching them to love themselves and value their self-worth and uniqueness. Then, by inspiring those children to love, accept and encourage everyone else to do the same, we will create peace on earth."

Krystalya Marié is an Empowerment Guide, Self-Love Enthusiast, Author and Speaker. EmpoweredSpirit.com

My Big Idea

— DAY 122—

My Big Idea

"Once you achieve balance in your life, then everything is possible. I'm not talking about just balance between work and personal life. I am talking about finding the balance between your masculine and feminine energies. Everyone has both. Male energy is warrior-like: hard, driven, hustle, logical, practical, and pushing. Feminine energy is goddess-like: soft, allowing, having faith, believing, forgiving, emotional, trusting intuition, listening to divine guidance and knowing all will work out as it should."

Kathy Mortenson, Intuitive/Psychic Business Coach for women entrepreneurs. Creator of Divine Business Academy, Public Speaker and Children's book Author in the making. KathyMortenson.com

My Big Idea

My Big Idea

— DAY 124—

"When overwhelm creeps in or you're unsure of your next steps, allow the creative spirit from within to guide you forward. Eliminate all distractions, find solitude, listen from within and take inspired action. Enjoy a nature hike, meditate, take a staycation or dust off that hobby project you've been dreaming of completing.

Amplify your life by aligning with one of my keys to opening doors easily = ABRA (Cadabra) is magic! Ask. Believe. Receive. Achieve."

Carrie Stepp is a Master Teacher, award-winning digital course designer, international best-selling author, inventor, and intuitive creator.   CarrieStepp.com

My Big Idea

My Big Idea

— DAY 125—

"To get to where you want to go, you need a plan. A plan needs steps. Steps need baby steps. Visualize the end result or keep a picture of something similar where you see it every day. Grab some determination and enthusiasm and mix with a huge chunk of motivation and you will get to your goal. Find a way to ignore the bitch in your head, as she is way too critical and will derail you every chance she gets."

Mary Coles is a Photographer, Horticulturist, Optician and wannabe Author. MaryColes@me.com

My Big Idea

— _DAY 125_—

My Big Idea

— DAY 126—

"True peace lies in the hearts of mankind. Being born with the milk of innocence, we are endowed with the gifts of love, harmony and peace. In order for peace to prevail within, you must allow your inner love to shine: love for the creator, the world and people therein. Release that warm palpable love inside and your sweet inner peace so that you can be at one with the universe. The world needs you!"

Desziree Richardson is an Int'l Best-Selling and Award-Winning Author, an experienced broadcaster, and Board Member of Bestselling Authors International Organization. Desziree.com

My Big Idea

— _DAY 126_—

My Big Idea

— DAY 127—

"If you are not feeling alive, are you truly living? So many people operate a definition of success that only allows them to feel good about life and themselves when they achieve something. If that's you, you are robbing and denying yourself the personal freedom to enjoy life. Life is your inheritance and life is now, so decide to embark on a transformational journey that allows you to thrive with powerful purpose now, not tomorrow!"

Anita Narayan is the Best-Selling Author of *Breaking Free*, Speaker, Freelance TV Presenter, CEO of Breaking Free Unlimited, which is dedicated to powerful transformation and inspirational legacy. BreakingFreeUnlimited.com

My Big Idea

My Big Idea

"The BEST you is in you and has been in you all along. You don't need to be more. You just need to unlock the BEST you by transforming your negative beliefs around 'Can I do this?' 'Am I good enough?' 'Do I deserve this?' and 'Am I worth it?' to 'Yes! I can! Yes I am MORE than enough! Yes! Yes!' When you shine through as your Happy.Positive.Successful self, your life of your dreams is yours to create and enjoy!"

Soochen Low, "Queen of Clearing Blocks to Joyful Living" is Happy.Positive.Successful Joy Expert & Coach, author, speaker and creator of the 5 Step Happy.Positive.Successful Formula. HappyPositiveSuccessful.com

My Big Idea

— *DAY 128*—

My Big Idea

— DAY 129—

"Live from your heart! Let others see your unique light that only you can shine. Embrace each day with child-like joy. Dare to be you! Remember, there's never been anyone else exactly like you and there never will be again. Celebrate yourself! Know you're meant to be here, at this time. Give it your all, the best you can! Practice self-care. Show others you care. And... Always let your Heart Light your Way!"

Karen Fitts Penaluna, Inspirational Writer, Heart-centered Intuitive, Positive Change Activist, Real Estate Entrepreneur & Sustainable Energy Entrepreneur.   KarenFittsPenaluna.com

My Big Idea

— _DAY 129_ —

My Big Idea

"A big idea is an idea in which you invest energy. Attention is key. 'Where attention goes, energy flows.' The necessary step is to just begin getting involved. The big idea in my life is related to music, and using music as a connector, a bridge, between the visible/material world and the world we cannot see. As I hear or play music, it is a gateway to focus on future steps. What is your gateway?"

Mary Azima Jackson, MDiv, DMin Azima's expertise focuses on life's rites of passage through song, meditation, and ceremony. She is an ordained Interfaith Minister with a Masters from Yale Divinity School. aHouseofLight.com

My Big Idea

— *DAY 130* —

My Big Idea

— DAY 131—

"Your physical body plays a significant role in your creativity. If you haven't slept well recently; if you haven't consistently eaten healthy food; or (most importantly) you haven't drunk enough water, your brain won't 'light up.' For a temporary fix to help you get over 'blank page syndrome' - if you've got to be creative RIGHT NOW - drink a large glass of water and move to some slightly upbeat instrumental music!"

Sue Wilhite, Author, Publisher and Creator of "The Sweet Sound of Sleep." SweetSoundofSleep.com

My Big Idea

My Big Idea

— DAY 132—

"What is 'impossible?' Born in the 1880s, my grandmother witnessed many 'impossible' inventions: electricity, telephone, plumbing, aspirin, penicillin, cars, airplanes, movies, radio, Man on the Moon, cable TV, and computers. 'Impossible' is a word used by critics who fail to visualize the possibility to achieve the impossible. Do not let fear and doubt steal your dreams. Nothing is impossible with a creative imagination, a strong will to succeed, and a plan of action!"

Rico Marciano, Author, Certified Physical Fitness Instructor, and Award-Winning Producer who's been featured on ABC, NBC, CBS, FOX, *The Palm Beach Post*, Clear Channel Radio. RicoWorldwide@aol.com

My Big Idea

My Big Idea

"One idea can transform a life. It can take you from broke and hopeless to inspired, passionate, and wealthy beyond conscious understanding. The secret lies in the power of our souls to whisper an idea that is our unique gift. Our challenge is to quiet the monkey mind, tame the reactive emotions to hear the message, and take action on the intuitive guidance. I accessed this truth through a near-death experience and pass this legacy to you."

Dr. Tianna Conte is a transformational best-selling author and trailblazing blend of mystic and scientist. With 40 years of expertise, she empowers self evolution by re-awakening innate guidance. InfinitePossibilitiesProductions.com

My Big Idea

— _DAY 133_ —

My Big Idea

— DAY 134 —

*"When you make decisions based on fear and scarcity, you keep yourself stuck and playing small. Fear is a mechanism designed to keep you **safe**. However when you make choices from faith and possibility, you align with your soul's deepest calling which allows you to **soar**. Even if your path seems uncertain, Life is for you and sets in motion a chain reaction of absolute good that must come to you! I declare it!"*

Lorna Blake, Best-Selling Author, International Speaker, Leadership Coach, Empowering Thousands Globally. MpowerUrself.com

My Big Idea

— DAY 134 —

My Big Idea

— DAY 135 —

"What if I said to you that you are perfect and beautiful just as you are? What if I said to you that you have everything you need to be a success? Would you look at your life experiences in a different way if you knew they were all part of a divinely perfect plan? What would you do with that knowledge? How could you use it to be of more service to the world?"

Mary Magouirk is a certified Law of Attraction Coach specializing in expanding the vision of what is beautiful in our world. CoachAltaGracia.com

My Big Idea

— *DAY 135* —

My Big Idea

"The most significant Aha is realizing that life doesn't happen To you, it happens For you. There's wisdom to be mined from every experience, whether windfall or wound. Asking: Truth: If X happened/is happening for my highest and best, what might that be? puts you into a space of gratitude for the wisdom you may not be able to see... yet. Approaching life with this outlook opens you to the infinite possibilities available to you."

Maureen Marie Damery, former Microsoft Programmer, Holistic Facilitator and Author of forthcoming book, *Your Owner's Manual for Life ~ Source Code of Your Soul.* BarnStoneHealing.com

My Big Idea

— _DAY 136_—

My Big Idea

— *DAY 137*—

"21 years old Joseph Schooling from Singapore made history when he beats his idol Michael Phelps to win the country's 1ˢᵗ Olympic Gold.

Be like Michael Phelps is his goal. He takes massive actions and pays the price to get there. He meets with failures but he is able to pick himself up, confront and learn from his failures. He keeps focus on the goal, persevere and results finally arrive."

GOAL – ACTIONS – FAILURES – FOCUS – RESULTS

Sam Chia is a passionate business and leadership coach who cares about your success.   SCCoachingAsia.com

My Big Idea

— _DAY 137_ —

My Big Idea

— DAY 138—

"Too many people limit their own success by stuffing their dreams into a tiny box. It's just about feeling safe by not stepping outside of these limits. You are too wonderful to stifle all that brilliance! Erase the self-limiting lines you draw and give yourself permission to stop containing your aspirations. Let them jump out and surprise not only yourself, but others. Each time you set your dreams free, they change your perspective for the better."

Tess C. Taylor, CCC, CPC, SHRM-CP is the Founder of HR Knows, a Best-Selling Author, and a Human Resources Professional and Career Coach. HRKnows1@gmail.com

My Big Idea

— _DAY 138_—

My Big Idea

— _DAY 139_—

"Become Your Own Legend and Leader ~ Have you ever noticed how all the leaders are legends? They are themselves. They hold themselves accountable for their actions. They follow their hearts, their dreams and their passions even if they have to do it alone. And that's when they become a legend. Take action, stay true to you, be accountable in your own heart and live your own dream. It's yours and yours alone to live."

Tanja Turner holds a Teaching Diploma, BA of Education, Masters of Education (Information Technology) and is a Neuro-Linguistic Programming Master Practitioner.
TanjaTurner.com

My Big Idea

— *DAY 139* —

My Big Idea

— DAY 140 —

*"Never confuse the power of love with the love of power. Love is boundless, unconditional. Filled with happiness, it cherishes, encourages, nurtures and supports your dreams; giving you the wings to fly. Power encroaches slowly. Little by little it steals your dreams, whittling your confidence and self-esteem away. It lives to take, embarrass, hurt, diminish and empty you; leaving but a pale shadow of your former self. You deserve so much more. **You deserve love.**"*

Stella Waterhouse is an Autism Awareness Expert and the author of the #1 Amazon best-selling book, *Autism Decoded: The Cracks in the Code.* AutismDecoded.com

My Big Idea

My Big Idea

"Believing in yourself is a strong component to personal growth, accomplishments and satisfaction. If you never throw the dart, you'll never hit the bulls-eye. Lessons learned come from chances taken. Some people achieve whatever it is they set their mind's eye on; others need a little motivation or an encouraging word to move forward in life. I know that you never really lose in life, only lessons learned that ultimately help develop the unique person you are today."

TC Franklin, Emmy-Nominated Journalist, Washington D.C. National TV News Correspondent, Author, Writer, Actor, Director, and Filmmaker. TCFranklinPhotography.com

My Big Idea

— _DAY 141_—

My Big Idea

— DAY 142 —

"Internetlivestates.com shows there are one billion+ websites on the internet and counting. Unfortunately, according to a Nielson estimate, most sites go unseen by the average person as they only visit 96 unique sites per month.

So how do you make your online presence stand out? **Video!** *Savvy marketers know there's no better way to convey your message, increase your brand awareness and develop relationships with your clients/potential clients then by incorporating video into your marketing."*

Mark Muller is a Speaker, Best-Selling Author and owner of LuxMark International, <u>LuxMarkInternational.com</u>, and New Media Ranch, <u>NewMediaRanch.com</u>.

My Big Idea

My Big Idea

— DAY 143 —

*"Life can knock you lower than a green grasshopper's knee. If you look UP, you will see the grasshopper in all its glory. Embrace its radiant beauty and iridescence as your guiding light, submitting to Love and Faith. Suddenly kaleidoscopic points of view and creative positions arise. Abundant opportunities grace your horizons. Faith rewards your loyalty, flinging doors open! Love renews Your Trust in Life and you sail into its unfolding. Hello **Magnificentia!**"*

Gaongalelwe Mosweu is a Creative, Speaker, Teacher, Writer, Bibliophile. Runs extraordinary consultancy company, solving ordinary business challenges. Volunteer for ICT4Development. Life story epitomizes *"beauty from ashes."* MazeMeadows.com

My Big Idea

My Big Idea

— DAY 144 —

"The spirit of gratitude shines away darkness and invigorates the flow of blessings in our lives.

We become more empowered accepting and transcending life's challenges by cultivating an incessant spirit of gratitude. As we embrace and nurture this sacred union with our true self, inner fulfillment with clarity and insight is achieved. It enhances our realization and appreciation that abundance in the universe is available to each of us."

Dr. Jean Farish, award-winning transformational author and Founder, Life Care Wellness/PEP For Angels for personal empowerment, community enrichment, and support for children with cancer.   jeanfarishjourney.com

My Big Idea

My Big Idea

— DAY 145 —

"It's no wonder we often feel overwhelmed in today's fast-paced and violent world. We are anxious travelers living in a strange land without a map. This is why learning about the Hero's Journey is so essential today. It provides us with a 4000 year old map we can follow to create our own Hero's Journey, a story to open our hearts and minds — and lift us out of the dark pit of powerlessness."

Kat Tansey is an expert at facilitating change who uses the magic of the Hero's Journey to help people transform their lives. Kat-Tansey.com

My Big Idea

My Big Idea

"We are living in a time of planetary transformation. We live in a time when everyone's gifts - large and small - are needed. What if, by taking a daily break from our digital devices, we could contribute to a greater harmony? **Stop.** For a moment, just be. **Look**. Take in the sights of the beauty around you. Share your smile with another. **Listen**. What does your heart whisper? Realize that YOU are the gift."

Francesca A. Jackson, DC is a workshop leader, speaker, best-selling author, and the founder of YinRise. YinRise.com

My Big Idea

— _DAY 146_—

My Big Idea

"Every day, and everything I do, is an experiment. I put things out and see what comes back. It's a way of living that consistently invites the world to interact with me. If you are not creating your life through experimentation, you are living your life through someone else's experiment that is done and gone – in the past. Open to the experiment of life and meet your divine creative self in everything you do."

Kaarin Alisa is a best-selling author, teacher, spiritual advisor, and practical metaphysician. She has worked with people from all lifestyles to find and embrace their best life. KaarinAlisa.com

My Big Idea

— *DAY 147*—

My Big Idea

— DAY 148—

"As a pageant girl, I have spent a lot of my time on stage waiting and praying for my name to be called. Many times my name would never be called so I would be left on stage holding back tears and forcing a smile... But I was still on stage - I still had the opportunity to grow and learn. Results are not as important when you can find value in the opportunity."

Megan Ashley Whited has been acting, modeling and competing in pageants for several years. She is currently the 2016 Royal International Miss Colorado.
MeganAshleyWhited.com

My Big Idea

— *DAY 148*—

My Big Idea

"When people would tell me, 'God has a reason for doing this to you,' I would respond, 'God did not do this to me, I am responsible for my own mistakes. If God had any part in this it was to keep me breathing during the half hour it took to get me freed from my automobile.' There may be a divine power that keeps you strong; there is not one that knocks you down."

Susanne Whited helps business owners escape the marketing madness to focus on practical solutions to grow their business by strategy consultations, educational programs and done-with-you services. <u>MyBusinessTweets.com</u>

My Big Idea

— _DAY 149_—

My Big Idea

"It took a cancer diagnosis to push me to start making a difference in the world. When you face a life-threatening illness, you're very much reminded of all the things you wanted to do with your life. Suddenly you wonder if you'll ever get to them, or if 'this is it.' Stop waiting for 'some day' and 'one day' because they never come. Step into your potential and live your best life, starting today."

Rosalind Cardinal - The Leadership Alchemist - Coach, Speaker, Facilitator and Organisational Development Specialist at Shaping Change. Author of bestseller, *The Resilient Employee*. RosalindCardinal.com

My Big Idea

— _DAY 150_—

My Big Idea

— DAY 151—

"Believe in your success and the power of your words. Have belief in the power of your plan. Take action to move your plan forward. If you find you went left and should have gone right, stop, remember your plan and turn around. All roads forward lead to your success. Success will come easy; it is longevity that takes time. Continue to overcome objections and obstacles; your success will grow. Believe, Act, Succeed, and Overcome!"

Charmagne Coston is a Motivational Speaker, Best-Selling Author and Owner of Branch Out Solutions, a business solutions and relationship building company.
BranchOutSolutions.com

My Big Idea

— *DAY 151*—

My Big Idea

— *DAY 152*—

"Like new lovers, there's nothing so intimidating and simultaneously enticing about a crisp blank page. It beckons our truths to spill out like secrets shared through afterglow pillow talk...

And like an insatiable lover, that page eagerly laps all that you're willing to share, embracing each word that comes...

After many years, good writing is like comfortable retirees who've stood the trying tests of time... writings that still endure like soulmates through pleasure and pain."

Best-selling, award-winning transformational author, women's empowerment consultant, and Winged~Women™ Founder, **Jan Deelstra** can be found most days, spilling secrets on the pages... JanDeelstra.com

My Big Idea

My Big Idea

— DAY 153—

"What if where I am now is the place I have to be... to see the next turn I was meant to make?

What if all the world was lining up in just this moment... to reveal how where I am is no mistake?

What if my love... won't wait?'
(Lyrics from my original song, 'What if.)

What gifts do you have that you have yet to share? How are you being invited to shine?"

Mark Olmstead is the Author of the first family keepsake coloring book, *The True Sunbeam*, and composer of the unofficial soundtrack to world peace, "One Peace at a Time." TrueSunbeam.com

My Big Idea

....
....
....
....
....
....
....
....
....
....
....
....
....
....
....
....
....
....
....

— _DAY 153_—

My Big Idea

"You play a unique part in the mighty orchestra of the universe. Not only are you a specific spark of the Divine, here to shine your facet of light into the world, but you also have a song in your soul. Isn't it time to free your creative spirit by crafting a piece of music and lyrics that represents you, your soul and your purpose? Discover the 6 Simple Steps to Creating YOUR Signature Soul Song!"

Lauren Perotti blends 32 years of expertise in business, psychology and expressive arts to guide spiritual seekers and lovers of life to design lives they love. <u>LaurenPerotti.com</u>

My Big Idea

My Big Idea

— DAY 155 —

"Henry Ford said, 'You can take my factories and burn up my buildings, but give me my people and I'll build the business right back again.' Why? Because Human resource is the most important source of power! As such, there is a need to make HR processes simple, efficient and effective. It will help to add value to the individual as well as organizational competencies. After all, whatever doesn't make business sense, cannot make HR sense!"

Ashok Grover, Human Resources Expert, Executive & Leadership Coach, Balanced Score Card Trainer & Implementation Support — helping professionals and companies to enhance their competencies.   Skillscape.net

My Big Idea

_____
_____
_____
_____
_____
_____
_____
_____
_____
_____
_____
_____
_____
_____
_____
_____

My Big Idea

— DAY 156 —

"These are moments in life where we have the opportunity to step out of who we believe we are and into a new version of ourselves, even if it scares the hell out of us ... take the chance! Are you holding on so tightly that you are not allowing a new you to emerge? To live a healthy and authentic life from the inside out, it all starts by YOU making the first choice. Are you ready?"

Peter Stanton is the Founder of Source Conditioning Health, Fitness and Vitality Centre.
facebook.com/Source-Conditioning-221251321227196/

My Big Idea

My Big Idea

— DAY 157—

"Life is good especially when you apply PMA - a positive mental attitude, which automatically eliminates complications, negativity, stress and worry. Even failure gets pushed into oblivion. To access your PMA, follow these simple guiding principles that guarantee you'll enjoy a happier and abundant lifestyle by design: **Plan** *your optimum lifestyle;* **Take** *action to activate your inner powerhouse;* **Review** *daily;* **Always** *keep your desired outcome in mind;* **Smile** *gracefully; then* **Begin** *today. You know you're worth it."*

PaTrisha-Anne Todd, award-winning Author, Publisher, Info-preneur, Speaker and Master Life Coach. Founder of 'Coaching Leads To Success' the on-line gateway for lifestyle success.   CoachingLeadsToSuccess.com

My Big Idea

— *DAY 157*—

My Big Idea

— DAY 158—

"Volunteering with 'Wounded Warriors,' I've discovered writing as therapy. Unexpressed painful memories and experiences may appear in your body as tension; writing can provide relief. This safe process coupled with professional support helps you to discover your "new normal" and transforms your life. To enjoy renewed courage, confidence, and release, start journaling today, without judgment or limits. To find a place in yourself that was never wounded, contact a trusted advisor to gain maximum support."

Cheri Sigmon, Cybersecurity, executive coaching and leadership expert with the Office of the Secretary of Defense, Joint Staff, and retired US Air Force officer.
ExecSec.LifeMasteryConsultant.com

My Big Idea

— _DAY 158_—

My Big Idea

— DAY 159 —

"Your unique gifts and skills are what the world needs most at this time of great change. Your creativity and your open mind are required for reaching for solutions beyond the known. So let your questions be bigger than your answers; let them be like open windows into new realities and into possibilities beyond your wildest imagination."

Metka Lebar, Founder of Foundation for Creative Thinking and Ecology of Mind, is a best-selling author, inspirational speaker, healer, workshop leader, consciousness facilitator, life and creativity coach.   facebook.com/AccessOneness/

My Big Idea

My Big Idea

— *DAY 160*—

"What is it that ultimately determines your experience of life? I've come to understand it's not the choices of others, untimely hardships, or even fortunate windfalls we receive. It's the perspective we choose to have and the desires of our heart.

Where one sees the devastation of a natural disaster, another recognizes an opportunity to serve and make a difference. Where one sees only lemons, another notices potential for a refreshing cup of lemonade."

Jason Westover, Speaker, Author, Co-founder of *Godmade Lemonade*, and Founder of <u>TurningPassionIntoProfits.com</u>, transforming people struggling to live a life of purpose and increase their income.

My Big Idea

— _DAY 160_—

My Big Idea

— DAY 161—

 *"If you have a passion, go for it. My high school art teacher discouraged me from pursuing art as a career based on his own experience as a struggling artist. To deny my passion would have been turning out the light in my soul. All forms of art is food for the soul. It is the inspiration that lifts humanity to whole new levels of understanding. When we follow our passion, we transform ourselves, others and the world."*

Rita Koivunen, Published and Award-Winning Artist, has been creating art for 45 years. A fun art class in high school became a lifelong inspirational journey. RitaKoivunen.com

My Big Idea

— DAY 161—

My Big Idea

— DAY 162—

*"Happiness is a choice, success is a mindset. The secret is knowing how to **leverage your mind**. You can train your brain to get what you want. Learn to align it with your subconscious, and with your heart and soul to **recognize your greatness**, your unlimited potential, unique skills and experiences. Then, **reset within** by reprogramming with only the positive perspective, always disregard negative thoughts and feelings. Lastly, you **reinvent yourself for results** through action."*

Luc Goulet, Author, Speaker, and "Leverage Your Mind" Coach. Founder of "The Big Bang Project," devoted in helping people who want to help themselves and others.
TheBigBangProject.com

My Big Idea

— _DAY 162_—

My Big Idea

— DAY 163—

"Charity, the pure love of Christ, for Motherhood is the noblest and holiest of callings women can have. Mothers have great influence on their children and are a foundation of love. The home resembles a laboratory of learning where everything she does and teaches affects the life of her child. By her leading, guiding and walking beside them, children gain characteristics that'll determine the life they'll live and the difference they'll make in the world."

Amber Westover, Coach, aspiring Author on How Too Love, Wife in an Amazing marriage, Mother of 3, and a National Board Certified Teacher.   SisterWestover@gmail.com

My Big Idea

_____

_____

_____

_____

_____

_____

_____

_____

_____

_____

_____

_____

_____

_____

_____

_____

_____

_____

My Big Idea

— DAY 164 —

"It's time to break the trance, challenge the status quo and engage critical thinking. With the simple 'Challenge. Solution. Invitation.' framework YOU can create marketing messages with integrity by focusing on PASSION points instead of pain points and building relationships. Simply acknowledge the challenge of your ideal clients, offer your solution with value proposition to empower your audience with the knowledge they need to ensure you're a natural choice when you gracefully extend your invitation."

Lisa Manyon is The Business Marketing Architect. Powerful solutions, profitable revenue streams and creating marketing messages with integrity as seen in *Inc. Magazine.* WriteOnCreative.com

My Big Idea

_____

_____

_____

_____

_____

_____

_____

_____

_____

_____

_____

_____

_____

_____

_____

_____

_____

_____

— _DAY 164_—

My Big Idea

— DAY 165 —

"What does being Successful mean to you? The meaning of success is different for everyone. Your passion, values, inspiration and effort will play a role, but in order to achieve true success, we must first discover what our greatest self looks and feels like then determine the steps needed to get there and finally take action! Be bold, be passionate, be heart centered!"

Cheryl Thacker, Master Board Certified Coach, Director Recovery Nation, Speaker and Trainer. Founder of Successful Coaches Enterprise, My Coach Supervisor and Coaching for Healthy Living.

My Big Idea

My Big Idea

— DAY 166—

"Brave is believing there is MORE, especially when fear is saying the opposite ... 'Not you, not now, not ever!' My recent poignant Life Lesson: 'There are always options!' It's time to rewrite your story that has been limiting how you see yourself. Your greatest power is the Power to Choose. Reach out for assistance to create the next chapter of your life. Work-Life Balance is an ebb and flow of Letting Go and Receiving."

Sally Holland, Life Coach to adults in Transition. Celebrating your difference. Re-Visioning your life purpose. Creative Solutions with Surprising Clarity.
KeepItSimpleSally.com

My Big Idea

— *DAY 166* —

My Big Idea

— DAY 167—

"My Big Idea is the Power of Intention, which has guided my life for the past 47 years. Through being totally focused on my goals, I have been able to achieve each and every one of them. There have even been times when the results have completely surpassed my wildest dreams. The process begins with focusing on the result and seeing it as already manifested and then staying totally focused and witnessing the miracle happen."

Bill McCarthy has been a special event producer for 47 years. He is also the Founder and President of Unity Foundation.   UnityFoundation.org

My Big Idea

My Big Idea

"Time for harmony in your life is now. Not later, not at the weekend. Now! You have the power of choice. So choose WISELY. Create harmony and balance in life Now!

Gently close your eyes. Feel the air coming through your nostrils. Give yourself permission to slow down. Allow yourself to stand still, listen and just... be. Open up your arms to receive love (because God loves you). You are enough. You... Are...

Perfect creation."

Kathleen Zajac, Divine Feminine Leader, Energy Healer, Meditation Teacher, Author of deeply healing guided meditations, Life Transformation Mentor for successful high achieving women entrepreneurs.   KathleenZajac.com

My Big Idea

_____
_____
_____
_____
_____
_____
_____
_____
_____
_____
_____
_____
_____
_____
_____
_____

— *DAY 168*—

My Big Idea

"When your website content doesn't engage, entertain and inspire your target audience, you are just writing words. Having content that brings your audience back for more is the only way to stand out in our fast paced world. By connecting their beautifully written stories with engaging online content, Romance Authors can more successfully inspire and entertain their following."

Shental Henrie, copywriter, content writer, and soon-to-be author. Helping Romance Authors offer their readers website content that is engaging, entertaining and inspiring.
RomanceCopywriter.com, RomanceCopywriter@gmail.com

My Big Idea

— *DAY 169* —

My Big Idea

"'Life design is about mindset, energy, self connection and conscious creation.'

Quantum Life Design Principles™ are the energetic, physical, mental, emotional and spiritual laws based on science that mold your life and hold the secret to success, happiness and health.

Your life will only be as brilliant as your management skills of these principles. The good news is that the knowledge and use of them will transform your reality in extraordinary ways!"

Ulrika Nilsson, Transformation expert, Certified Int'l Coach, Certified Quantum Life Coach, Certified Energy Healer, Bachelor in Holistic Health Sciences, Innovator and former Hotel Manager. Ulrika-Nilsson.com

My Big Idea

— _DAY 170_—

My Big Idea

— DAY 171 —

"Age should not define your passion. Some people think that they will never reach their dreams because people tell them they are too old or too young. You are never too young or too old to follow your dreams. Never give up what you love. Age is just a number. Don't let that stop you from chasing your dreams and doing the things that you love the most."

Mikaila Hanzelka is an author, blogger, and entrepreneur who started her own business at the age of 14 despite others telling her she was too young.   mikailahanzelka@gmail.com

My Big Idea

— _DAY 171_—

My Big Idea

"Follow your dreams. No matter how big they may be. No matter how far away they seem. No matter how much you feel like you can't achieve them. For one of the things we fear the most is not failure, but greatness to do extraordinary things beyond our wildest imagination—to do the things we're created to do. And for that, we must let nothing stand in our way."

Nathanael Hanzelka loves life and is passionate about creating his own music. As a young entrepreneur he is a website designer and audio engineer.
nathanaelhanzelka@gmail.com

My Big Idea

— DAY 172—

My Big Idea

"Knowing your WHY is powerful! It enables you to focus your efforts on what matters most in life. It empowers you to push forward regardless of obstacles. Knowing your WHY will give you a compelling goal, laser like focus, clarity and confidence as you tap into your potential and the unique gifts that you have. You will know you've found your WHY when it becomes a mission. Be a more powerful you. KNOW YOUR WHY!"

Marlene Hanzelka, Reset Warrior, Success Coach, Author and Co-Founder of The Reset Formula; a formula to empower others to become the best they can be.   ResetYourView.com

My Big Idea

— *DAY 173*—

My Big Idea

— *DAY 174*—

"Your time is so precious. When you suffer a setback, which may be bereavement, relationship difficulty, a sudden unexpected event, it can throw you off course. You need time to deal with this but soon you approach what I call the 'crossroads.' You have three choices; straight on where you continue to suffer, left turn to be beset with problems or the right turn to recovery and moving on with your life. Be inspired turn right!"

Doug Marshall, owner of fledgling company Tiger Personal and Business Development aiming to help others through his own experience of overcoming personal setbacks.
TigerPandBd@outlook.com

My Big Idea

— *DAY 174* —

My Big Idea

"'Good, better, best. Never let it rest. 'Til your good is better and your better is best.'
~St. Jerome

This quote reminds me that GOOD is good enough, but BEST is what we should all aspire to. Best does NOT mean perfect. We all become better with practice and we're not expected to get it right the first time. It's a growing process. Everyone's goal should be to become the best version of themselves."

Paula Webb is an author living in Texas. A self-proclaimed lifelong learner, she believes everyone has a story to tell.
Paula@PaulaWebbHome.com

My Big Idea

— _DAY 175_—

My Big Idea

— DAY 176 —

*"Your success is not because you have all of your ducks in a row or having that special endorsement. Your success started when what you do began to change, uplift a community, nation and sector. 'YOU ARE SUCCESSFUL' because you are living in the purpose you were born for. Keep being and doing **you**. When God created you, He anointed, chose and formed **you**. Now go and reach for the stars because 'YOU already are one'!"*

Chantay Bridges is a dynamic Realtor, Coach, Writer and Speaker. As a noted Expert Chantay has empowered the masses being featured nationwide over 100 times! LosAngelesRealEstateNow.com

My Big Idea

_____

_____

_____

_____

_____

_____

_____

_____

_____

_____

_____

_____

_____

_____

_____

_____

_____

_____

_____

My Big Idea

— DAY 177—

"Shangri-love is found deep within your heart. It is a completely self-sustaining place within you and it requires nothing external for its sustenance, maintenance, or attainment. It's that part of you that is the lotus flower blooming in whatever mud life produces. It's the soul stamina that anchors you in joy. Shangri-love is your awakened radiant heart. It's universal and you have the power to access it."

Zemirah Jazwierski, Ed.S., RSCP, an empowerment coach, psychologist, licensed spiritual practitioner, meditation facilitator. Author of the book, *Shangri-love: Living The Love Story Within You*. Shangri-Love.com KidsRelaxation.com

My Big Idea

— DAY 177 —

My Big Idea

— DAY 178 —

"These days we rarely take conscious time, letting time take us instead. We need islands of stillness to pause and be, not just do. It's in the stillness we find center, and in center we find self.

Rather than get caught in the frantic rush of time try pausing instead, exhaling long and slow ... look around with curiosity and a smile, and then return, reset and refreshed, to wherever you left off moments before."

Beverly Kune is a Mind-Body Integrative Therapist and Self-Empowerment Coach helping others find joy and emotional freedom in their lives. WholeSelfHealing.biz

My Big Idea

My Big Idea

— *DAY 179*—

"If you ask children all over the world what they want to be when they grow up, their answers will be as varied as the cultures they live in. I can guarantee you, however, that not one of them will tell you that all they want to do is pay bills and die. That would be ridiculous! But how many of us are living that very life? What's your dream? Why aren't you living it?"

Livia Nicole Andrade is a coach, speaker, author, wife, homeschooling mom of six and Oma of two...joyfully living a life more abundant. LivAbundantly.com

My Big Idea

My Big Idea

"From my perspective, if you automate everything by using technology and other people as a replacement layer for <u>your own</u> personal interaction with both your Ideal Audience™ (i.e. prospects) and especially your Ideal Advocates™ (i.e. prospective partners), you actually begin dehumanizing relationships. And, these key relationships that you once attracted begin to realize that you're dis-connected from them and they begin to dis-connect themselves from you."

TR Garland teaches Speakers, Authors, Coaches, & Service-Based professionals how to get more Prospects, Partners, Platforms, Publicity, & Positioning... using their FREE LinkedIn Profile.   LinkedInSpecialReport.com

My Big Idea

— *DAY 180*—

My Big Idea

— DAY 181—

*"A life without **Joy** is a life that feels hard and wasted. Joy in your life each day is as simple as thinking of things that make you happy: the sound of your kids laughing as you tickle them, the smell of a freshly mown lawn, the waves crashing on the beach, the sun in your face. Include or visualize them in your day every day. It's that simple and it's Free! Fill every day with **Joy!**"*

Joy Fairhall is the Founder of Mind Body Joy and Creator of 3 Minutes to Calm™ and How to Fill your heart with Joy™ methods. MindBodyJoy.com.au

My Big Idea

— DAY 181 —

My Big Idea

— DAY 182—

"Humans have the power of choice whereas animals and plants do not. We can choose to be healthy, happy and successful. We can choose to do good for our own self and the world. We can choose to live life to the fullest in Truth, Goodness with Beauty. Choose, decide, and take action! Then, simply sit back and watch all the magic happen!"

Vicki Tuong Vi Eaton, Founder: Healing H.A.P.P.Y. Bubbles Systems™, Complete Wellness Network LLC. Author of *Eternal Youth Secrets: How to Have Beautiful Hair, Glowing Skin at Any Age.*   <u>CompWellness.org</u>

My Big Idea

— _DAY 182_—

My Big Idea

— DAY 183—

"The hand we are dealt in life is never the one we envisioned for ourselves, but with the grace of God, we can learn to play it with joy, peace, and prosperity! It is not the challenges we face that define us. It is the way we respond to them. Each day when we wake up, we have a choice to make. Will we choose to focus on our problems, fears and regrets or on what we are grateful for?"

Drew Hunthausen is a survivor of bacterial meningitis at age 11. He woke up from a 3-month long coma totally blind and hearing impaired. Drew@NoExcusesBlindGuy.com DrewsInspirations.com

My Big Idea

— _DAY 183_—

My Big Idea

— DAY 184—

"If you were blessed to see today, to take one more breath, to pick up and read this book, you can still Be the You you've always dreamed you could Be. Action is necessary. Dreamers must become Doers to fulfill their Divine purpose in their life time. Become a Doer! Decide the first action step to make your Dream a reality and Do It Now!!!"

Tamia Dow, international motivational speaker, trainer, mentor, author and coach. She is currently working on her fifth book about living life to the fullest. TamiaDow.com

My Big Idea

My Big Idea

"You don't have to have a passion. You don't have to be excellent at anything. But you must be comfortable and accepting of who you are. Once you do that, the world will be a better place for you having been here."

Dane Russo received his Ph.D. in psychology from the University of Texas and worked at NASA for 38 years. He is retired and lives with his wife Jean in Manzanillo, Mexico. bbcards46@hotmail.com

My Big Idea

— _DAY 185_—

My Big Idea

"If anyone in your life is unwilling to treat you with the love and respect you deserve, you have the right to end your relationship with that person. Family, friend, parent or child, it simply doesn't matter who they are or their relationship to you. No one gets a free pass to mistreat you. Love yourself enough to ask them to stop and value your-self enough to walk away if they don't. You deserve better."

Jen Halulko is certified life coach, wife, and mom of 3 who teaches moms how using their creativity can help them have the happier, more satisfying lives they want. JenHalulko.com

My Big Idea

_____

_____

_____

_____

_____

_____

_____

_____

_____

_____

_____

_____

_____

_____

_____

_____

_____

_____

_____

_____

_____

— _DAY 186_—

My Big Idea

"Plato said every trait has a deficiency and an excess but balanced in the middle is ideal. He called it the 'Golden Means.' If Passive is the deficiency, Aggressive is the excess but Assertive is balanced. Balance is empowering. It empowers us without depriving others of their balance. The more we practice finding balance, the stronger it becomes. The stronger our balance, the more harmony, peace, joy and love flow into our lives... and that is GOLDEN!"

Joe Murphy, Entrepreneur, Student of life and Founder of the "Game Changers," guiding and empowering people in shifting their perception from survive to thrive. LivingFullTilt.com

My Big Idea

— _DAY 187_—

My Big Idea

— DAY 188—

"Persistence is essential for success. When you are working towards a goal or outcome you desire, you must be persistent. I say, 'Put your head down and power through.' Yes, it may be hard; you may falter and want to throw your hands up. DO NOT give up! Finish then bask in the wonderful feeling of accomplishment and satisfaction. Know that because of your persistence, you are and can continue to be successful!"

Pam Murphy is an entrepreneur who empowers her clients to create their ideal businesses by removing the obstacles blocking their way.   pamurphy49@yahoo.com

My Big Idea

— *DAY 188*—

My Big Idea

— *DAY 189*—

"A good leader should be a mentor, and I've always tried to be that. I had mentors who helped me through my early years, giving me the experience necessary to proceed. I try to share that with the team members with whom I work. Bounce innovative ideas off of them, see what their reaction is, and then listen to what they are saying. I always respected the team members' ideas and their competence — they were very bright individuals. I listened to what they had to say."

Terry Zweifel, Aerospace Engineer, #1 Int'l Best-Selling Author, responsible for 23 patents for safe air travel.
TerryZweifel.com

My Big Idea

— *DAY 189*—

My Big Idea

ALSO FROM
EXPERT INSIGHTS
PUBLISHING

#1 International Best-Selling Books:

Become a Bestseller and PR Magnet
Beyond Your Book
Birthing Your Book
Cancer: From Tears to Triumph
My Big Idea Book
My Big Idea Workbook
My Creative Ideas Journal
Ready, Aim, Captivate!
Ready, Aim, Excel!
Ready, Aim, Impact!
Ready, Aim, Influence!
Ready, Aim, Inspire!
Ready, Aim, Soar!
Ready, Aim, Thrive!
Tail Waggin' Tales
Wounded? Survive! Thrive!!!

Award-Winning Magazines:

Insights Magazine
PUBLISHED! Magazine
Stress Free Magazine
Resources Uncovered Magazine

About Expert Insights Publishing

Our mission is to give authors a voice and a platform on which to stand. We specialize in books covering innovative ways to meet the personal and business challenges of the 21st century.

Through our signature, inexpensive publishing and marketing services, we help authors publish and promote their works more effectively and connect to readers in a uniquely efficient system.

We employ an experienced team of online marketing strategists, ad copywriters, graphic artists, and Web designers whose combined talents ensure beautiful books, effective online marketing campaigns at easily affordable rates, and personal attention to you and your needs.

**We have promoted over 900 authors
to bestseller status.
Will you be next?**

Learn more about our current publishing opportunities at:

ExpertInsightsPublishing.com

Made in the USA
Middletown, DE
24 September 2023